Mad About

Raspberries & Strawberries

Other books in this series:

MAD ABOUT PASTAS & CHEESE
MAD ABOUT FISH & SEAFOOD
MAD ABOUT MUSHROOMS

Other books by Jacqueline Hériteau:

GROW IT, COOK IT
A FEAST OF SOUPS
ORIENTAL COOKING THE FAST WOK WAY
HOW TO GROW AND CAN IT

Mad About

Raspberries & Strawberries

by Jacqueline Hériteau

illustrations by Woodleigh Hubbard

A GD/Perigee Book

Perigee Books
are published by
The Putnam Publishing Group
200 Madison Avenue
New York, New York 10016

Typeset by International Computaprint Corp.

Library of Congress Cataloging in Publication Data

Hériteau, Jacqueline.
Mad about raspberries & strawberries.

Includes index.
1. Cookery (Raspberries) 2. Cookery (Strawberries) I. Title.
TX813.R37H47 1984 641.6′471 83-23689
ISBN 0-399-50994-1

First Perigee printing, 1984

Printed in the United States of America

1 2 3 4 5 6 7 8 9

Cover recipes include:
(front) Strawberry Cream Pie, page 46;
(back) Raspberry Tarts; Orange Cup with Berries, page 20; Raspberry Orange Soup, page 23; Rhubarb-Strawberry Marmalade, page 63;
Flowers Designed by Hunter Flowers, Park Avenue, New York City.

CONTENTS

Food makes happiness. The MAD ABOUT books are about the fun of cooking your favorite foods—the joy of sharing new and interesting foodscapes, the satisfaction of binging—tastefully. The philosophy of the series is that when you start with ingredients that you love—raspberries and strawberries, cream, fresh fruits, liqueurs—and the very best recipe, you and those who dine at your table are bound to have a wonderful time. If you cook to relax as well as to eat but don't have hours a day to shop and hover over the stove, you'll truly appreciate the MAD ABOUT approach to cuisine. You will find valuable general information on the next few pages.

Introduction 6
Growing your own 6
How to buy berries 8
Success every time: Preparing, preserving, freezing 9

Fresh, fresh, fresh fruits 10: from fresh fruit with CHOCOLATE-ORANGE FONDUE and WILD STRAWBERRIES WITH CRÈME FRAÎCHE to STRAWBERRY MANGO CREAM, and RASPBERRY SOUP.

The ice cream parlor 24: from BANANA SPLIT and RASPBERRY PARFAIT to STRAWBERRY ICE CREAM and frozen shakes and flips.

Berries 'n' cream 34: from COEUR À LA CRÈME and fruit fools to BAVARIAN CREAM and STRAWBERRY SHORTCAKES.

The pastry shop 42: from RASPBERRY ANGEL CAKE and STRAWBERRY CREAM PIE to RASPBERRY TARTS, and FLAKY PASTRY.

Berry boutique 50: specialties from RASPBERRY PANCAKES with a hot strawberry sauce to fritters, soufflés, and a chocolate-dipped strawberry centerpiece for parties.

The berry fairy 58: from RASPBERRY JAM and BAR-LE-DUC to RHUBARB-STRAWBERRY MARMALADE.

Recipe list 64.

SO PRETTY! SO GOOD!

Raspberries and strawberries are the prettiest of all the fruits, fragrant (strawberries are *Fragaria*, and related to roses), delicious, capricious. They have been loved by lovers, kings, queens, craftsmen, and artists since the world was young. Celebrated in poem and song. Worn as a coat of arms. Fought over. Applauded. Traded on the stock exchange. Cherished by children. Sought after by bears.

It is a fact that wild strawberries and clotted cream (Fraises des Bois, Crème Fraîche, page 14) is the most revered dessert in France (more than *profiteroles*—cream puffs). Only a handful of insider restaurants are able to commandeer the little wild berries for a select clientele. In Manhattan, hostesses still consider a sterling silver bowl filled with raspberries at least as celebratory as champagne.

The berries that decorate coats of arms and historic tapestries are wild fruits. It wasn't until the 1700s that the small strawberries cultivated in Italy, France, and England were crossed with larger natives from America and the berry we love was born. The ancient Romans picked wild raspberries. Their most famous naturalist, Pliny, wrote about them. The big raspberry we know got started in the 1600s and it is hardy! Varieties of the raspberry genus, *Rubus*, grow wild almost to the Arctic Circle, and are a staple of people who live in remote areas of the planet. But strawberries are almost as durable as raspberries. Dozens of plants have lived through droughty, hot summers in tubs on my Manhattan terrace, producing fruit as merrily as if they lived in a cool garden.

GROWING YOUR OWN BERRIES

You can grow your own raspberries: All you need is a sunny garden. They are produced on brambly bushes that sprawl and spread, need pruning to produce at their best, and require slightly acid soils. Planting time in the Northeast is early spring and, further south, in late winter. Each spring, fertilize with a handful of 5-10-5 per plant. Put in twelve bushes of an everbearing variety;

these produce heavily once or twice a year and give a few fruits in between. About pruning: ask your local Agricultural Extension agent for recommendations.

Growing strawberries is less demanding. You can do it on a big scale with standard-size plants in your backyard. Or you can grow a few dozen plants, standard sizes and *fraises des bois,* in containers and baskets anywhere there is sun. You need two or three dozen plants to make a meaningful crop. Strawberries are low-growing little creepers that send out runners all around, hoping to make berry babies in every direction—even downward from hanging baskets. The leaves are pretty, and when the berries ripen, they glow like tiny hobgoblins among the foliage. That makes them candidates for space in sunny borders of flower and vegetable gardens and around tubbed plantings on terraces. You can try a few *fraises des bois* plants indoors in a very sunny window—with luck and lots of watering, you may get a few little fruits.

Plant strawberries in early spring, as soon as the ground can be worked. Keep the flowers picked the first year—they'll remind you of simple-petaled roses, the briars that smell so heavenly in spring. That prevents the plants from setting fruit and helps them become established. The crop begins the second year, and it should be great.

Cut off the runners trying madly to root, except for a few you might want to encourage in order to have more berry plants. A starter strawberry garden of three dozen plants can quickly become as large as you wish, since each plant sends out several runners each year. Once a baby plant on its runner has rooted and put out a few more leaves, sever it from its parent, fertilize the area, watch it with Tender Loving Care, water as needed, and the following year you can plant this gift from the berry fairy. After six years, berry patches are ready for retirement.

Set the plant in the ground so the crown is neither higher nor lower than the level at which it was growing before. Sun must not strike the roots while you are planting. Mulch strawberries when the temperature goes into the low 20s, but not before. A cover of 6 inches of straw is ideal. The berries grow close to the ground and, I believe, got their name from the straw mulches applied to keep the berries clean.

HOW TO BUY BERRIES

Strawberries, like many fruits, have a wonderful fragrance when they are ripe and headily flavored. So sniff before you buy. Pass up the berries shaped like a cockscomb that appear on the market in late winter. The really tasty berries come in June and July. These round little dears, vulnerable garden varieties from local growers, are not nearly so queenly as the big reds, but they are more flavorful.

You also can tell a good berry by its color—brilliant red—and by its sheen. Strawberries become dull and dark when they are overripe, on their way to berry heaven. Check berry boxes—they tell tales. They will tell your nose of mildew and mold, which sour berries. Stains on the box indicate overripe berries losing their juice. Try to see the bottom layer of berries. The underripe ones get tucked in there by not-too-honest hands. Those berries won't ripen, and they have little flavor. If you get a box like that, make a sweet sauce, like the one on page 13, to flavor the underripe berries. Another check point is the stems. Wilted stems indicate tired berries.

Raspberries are sold stems off, unlike strawberries, because when the stems stay on raspberries, it means they aren't ripe for picking and, in fact, are too difficult to pick. Raspberries are more perishable than strawberries; that's why they are prohibitively expensive in urban markets. In Manhattan, the very best way to acquire raspberries at a reasonable price is to drive to Guilford, Connecticut, and pick them yourself at Bishops Farm Market in late August and September. Other cities are bound to have pick-them-yourself farms; search out one in your area. Berry picking is great fun!

Pick berries in the early part of the day, or in the later part of the afternoon. They taste best when a little warm from the sun.

The first raspberries to arrive in May are dark red, and just a little sugar turns them to ambrosia. In late summer, the berries are bigger, brighter in color, and plentiful enough to make jam–also less likely to mold and be overripe in the box. Before you buy either, shamelessly sniff the box for a hint of true raspberry perfume and avoid those showing juice stains. Raspberries are *so* delicate and they really haven't yet bred a travel-proof berry.

SUCCESS EVERY TIME: PREPARING, PRESERVING, FREEZING

When you get your exquisitely fragrant, absolutely perfect basket of berries home, spread the berries at once on a tray so they can have air. They are faint from overcrowding. Discard spoiled berries, and store the tray in the refrigerator. Rinse berries when you are ready to use them. Don't rinse unless you must. Most berries are clean. Some strawberries have so many seeds that some need to be rinsed away. Rinse berries under cold running water very briefly. Don't soak. Hull them after rinsing, not before. Drain in a roomy colander and spread them on paper towels to air-dry out of the sun. If you have rinsed the berries and don't, after all, use them, make them into sauce—they will be less than perfect tomorrow. Don't keep berries overnight, if possible. Buy and use them fresh!

Berries taste best at room temperature—warm enough to be fragrant. (Much of our sense of taste is actually a sense of smell.) So refrigerate berries only if the room is hot and the berries won't be used for many hours.

Always taste one berry from a lot before you start to cook with the others. Sweetness varies. If they seem especially tart to you, add the maximum amount of sugar called for. You can save berries, particularly tasteless strawberries, by adding lemon, orange, or pineapple juice and fruit pieces or by adding liqueurs—Grand Marnier, Cointreau, as described on page 13 for Strawberry Sauce. (Be aware that these liqueurs have an alcohol content.) Sugar is the big berry saver. As a rule, I add 2 to 3 tablespoons of sugar to a pint of berries, depending on their tartness.

Quantities to buy: Berries are sold by the pint in the familiar green plastic or pressed cardboard boxes. These containers hold two cups. There are half-pint boxes and quart (2 pint) boxes, priced to reflect their contents. The pint boxes hold 2 cups of strawberries—about sixteen big berries—and a scant 2 cups of raspberries. Two cups of berries, crushed, yield about 1 cup of puree.

Freezing berries: Berries freeze with ease. Sprinkle them with sugar, and if you plan to hold them a long time in the freezer, sprinkle with ascorbic acid also (the package will say how much). Or pack with a syrup made of 1 to 2 cups sugar dissolved in 4 cups water. Maintain in a freezer at 0° and use within the year.

FRESH, FRESH, FRESH

CHOCOLATE-ORANGE FONDUE WITH STRAWBERRIES

Preparation time: 15 minutes **Serves 4–6**

Strawberries and raspberries warm from the garden (or cool from the supermarket) are heaven when really ripe—that bursting red that yields juice almost at a glance. The perfect way to serve them is alone (strawberries with stems on): rinsed, drained, and chilled, with a mound of sugar and a puff of sweetened whipped cream on the side. Another glorious way is dipped in a heavenly chocolate fondue. Flavored with brandy, the alcohol cooks out. The "fondue pot" in the recipe can be any small, long-handled saucepan kept warm over an alcohol lamp or electrically. Fondue forks are used to skewer the fruits and dip them into the bubbling liquid. They are slender, long-handled forks, but a dinner fork will do.

- 4 tablespoons heavy cream
- 4 ounces (4 double squares) unsweetened chocolate
- 3/4 cup sugar, or more
- Pinch of salt
- 2 tablespoons raspberry brandy
- 1 tablespoon Cointreau
- 2 tablespoons gin
- 2 tablespoons butter
- Grated rind of 1/2 orange
- 1 pint strawberries
- 2 good eating oranges
- 2 ripe bananas

In a small heavy saucepan over low heat, heat the cream and melt the chocolate in it, stirring with a whisk until the sauce thickens—about 5 minutes. Beat in the sugar, salt, liqueurs, gin, and butter, and stir until shiny. Grate the rind of half an orange into the sauce, stir, and turn off the heat. Taste. If you prefer sweeter chocolate, add more sugar.

Rinse, drain, and air-dry the berries. Hull only if the stems are wilted. Heap in the center of a serving platter. Peel all the pitch from the oranges; peel the bananas. Slice both into thick chunks and place around the berries. Briefly reheat the chocolate, pour into a fondue pot if available, and serve with the fruit.

RASPBERRIES AND THICKENED CREAM

Preparation time: 10 minutes **Serves 4**

When you have fresh, ripe, perfumed raspberries, they should be served at room temperature, on silver, with a little thick cream. Ummmm!

- 1 pint raspberries
- 1/2 pint heavy cream
- 3 tablespoons sour cream
- Sugar

Don't rinse the raspberries unless they really have dirt clinging to them. If you do rinse them, do it quickly with cold water, drain at once, and scatter on paper towels to air-dry. Stir the heavy cream into the sour cream and let rest at room temperature. Serve the berries in glass dessert cups, and offer thickened cream and sugar with them.

STRAWBERRIES WITH RASPBERRY SAUCE

Preparation time: 10 minutes
Chilling time: 30 minutes or more **Serves 4**

This is an elegant dessert for company. Serve it in tall sherbet glasses so the extraordinary richness of the two shades of red shows up. A twist of orange peel—just the orange part—makes a pretty garnish, too.

- 1 pint strawberries
- 1 recipe Raspberry Sauce (p. 12)
- 4 tip sprigs fresh mint (optional)

Rinse the strawberries, hull and drain them, and slice into halves or quarters according to size, dividing the berries among dessert cups or sherbet glasses. Pour the Raspberry Sauce over the berry halves, and chill for 30 minutes or more. Garnish with sprigs of mint if you wish.

Variation: Pears in Raspberry Sauce—Serve Raspberry Sauce over drained, canned pear quarters, or over peeled, cored, quartered, ripe fresh pears.

RASPBERRY SAUCE WITH LIQUEURS

Preparation time: 5 minutes **Yield: 2–2 1/2 cups**

Ripe raspberries pureed with the sugar called for here have an intense flavor that rarely needs doctoring. To enhance the sauce, add liqueurs—but be aware that uncooked liqueur adds alcohol to the sauce. Berry sauces are marvelous over other berries, sliced bananas, leftover cakes, and ice cream.

- 2 pints raspberries
- 6 tablespoons sugar
- 2 tablespoons each gin and Cointreau (optional) or 3 tablespoons frozen orange juice concentrate plus 1 tablespoon grated orange rind

Rinse, drain, and hull the berries. Puree them in a food processor or a blender, or mash by hand, with the sugar. Add the gin and liqueurs or the orange concentrate and rind.

Variation: Grapes and Blueberries with Berry Sauce—Combine 1/2 pint washed, air-dried blueberries with 1/2 pound seedless green grapes and divide among four dessert cups. Put a generous tablespoon of sour cream over the berries in each cup, and divide 1 cup Raspberry Sauce over the desserts. Chill.

SOUR CREAM SAUCE

Preparation time: 5 minutes **Yield: 2 cups**

I am mad about whipped cream with berries, and I am equally mad about sour cream with berries!

- 1 pint sour cream
- 1 tablespoon sugar

Stir the sour cream and sugar together, and let stand a few minutes before serving.

STRAWBERRY SAUCE

Preparation time: 20 minutes
Marinating time: 1–2 hours **Yield: 2–2 1/2 cups**

Strawberries have a less intense flavor than raspberries. When they are just-picked berries bursting with flavor, adding sugar and lemon juice turns them into a delicious sauce. If the sauce is a little pale, add just a drop or two of red food coloring. When the berries are ahead of their season, they can be pretty tasteless. These you may enhance with liqueurs. (Be aware that liqueur that is uncooked has an alcohol content that is not pleasing to everyone.) For a fabulous, really fabulous *cooked* strawberry sauce, see page 51.

2 pints strawberries
1/4 cup sugar
1/8 cup fresh lemon juice
Pinch of salt

Rinse, drain, and hull the berries, and select about 1 pint of the least ripe ones. Puree these in a food processor or a blender or mash by hand, with the sugar, lemon juice and salt. Into the puree quarter or halve (depending on size) the remaining berries, reserving a few for garnish. Cover and chill for an hour or two or overnight before serving.

Variations: Strawberry Sauce with Liqueurs—For the lemon juice in the basic recipe, substitute Kirsch, Cointreau, and/or gin and add a tablespoon of orange juice concentrate. Or flavor to taste with Grand Marnier.

Grape and Sour Cream Cup with Berry Sauce—Divide 1 pound washed, air-dried, seedless green grapes among four dessert cups; divide 1/2 pint sour cream over them, and then divide 1 cup Strawberry Sauce among the cups. Chill before serving.

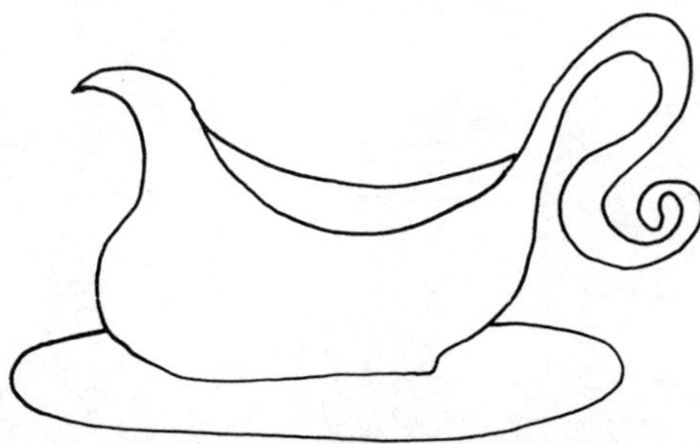

WILD STRAWBERRIES WITH CRÈME FRAÎCHE

Preparation time: 10–20 minutes **Serves 4**

Have you ever gathered the tiny, pointed little berries the French consider one of the great delicacies? We have found them covering hilly fields in southern Ontario and in Vermont. They take hours to pick and hull, but the fragrance is heavenly, and no cultivated berry quite equals them. Many garden catalogs offer *fraises des bois,* which is what the French call wild strawberries—strawberries of the woods, literally. They make exquisite borders on flower beds, and providing the beds face south and get lots of sun, the little plants will produce fruit generously through late spring, with some berries ripening now and then during the rest of the season—nice for garnishing fruit desserts. With these elegant little berries the restaurateurs in France offer Crème Fraîche—cream thick as it used to be in farm kitchens in Grandmother's day.

3–4 cups wild strawberries
2 cups Crème Fraîche (p. 15)
Extrafine granulated sugar

Hull the berries, rinse them in a little cold water, drain well, and air-dry on paper towels. Put in a serving bowl and offer with Crème Fraîche and a bowl of extrafine granulated sugar.

Variations: Raspberries with Crème Fraîche—Taste the berries, and add enough sugar to sweeten them. Just sprinkle it over the surface of the berries and let it sit. Serve with a dollop of Crème Fraîche.
Blueberries and Crème Fraîche—Sugar the berries, as suggested above for raspberries, and serve with Crème Fraîche.

CRÈME FRAÎCHE

Preparation time: 5 minutes
Setting time: 2–3 hours **Serves 4–6**

Crème fraîche is also called crème double, and today in Manhattan it is sold by fine food shops such as Dumas, the great pastry and bread store. It is fresh cream in which the lactic acids have been allowed to work until the cream will almost hold a spoon upright it is so thick. It has a slightly nutty flavor and won't curdle when boiled, unlike our heavy cream. If you can find crème fraîche, try it with berries and pastas. For fruit and other sweet desserts, I dilute commercial crème fraîche with heavy cream until the consistency is just right. I serve it without sugar, counting on the sweet, sharp flavor of the ripe fruit for sweetening. When I can't get crème fraîche, I make the substitute that follows and really like it almost as well. (Julia Child, in *Mastering the Art of French Cooking,* Knopf, 1967, suggests yet another way to make crème fraîche, and that is by heating a little buttermilk with heavy cream, then leaving the mixture to thicken for about twelve hours.)

- 1/2 pint heavy cream
- 1/2 pint sour cream

Combine the two creams and let thicken at room temperature 2 to 3 hours. Chill before serving.

Variation: Crème Fraîche with Saffron—Mix 1/4 teaspoon of saffron threads with the heavy cream before you combine it with the sour cream. Stir in enough sugar to sweeten, 1 or 2 tablespoonfuls, and let thicken, as recommended above. This is elegant with exotic fruits that are tart, such as drained, canned Mandarin oranges, and pineapple chunks.

PINEAPPLE BOATS STUFFED WITH STRAWBERRIES

Preparation time: 20 minutes
Chilling time: 30–60 minutes **Serves 4**

This is a party dessert that can't fail as long as the fruit is ripe. One test for pineapple is the ease with which a leaf can be pulled from the top. But acid green pineapple sometimes is remarkably willing to let leaves go. So instead, sniff for fragrance. Don't settle for anything less perfect than a yellow or red-gold fruit that smells so sweet you'd think someone had been distilling pineapple perfume. But beware of too-soft fruit that carries a whiff of fermenting fruit—it is too ripe. Three pineapples and 3 pints of berries will serve 14 to 16 guests. The boats make pretty centerpieces.

- 1 pint strawberries, rinsed and hulled
- 2 tablespoons sugar
- 1 ripe fresh pineapple
- 2 tablespoons Cointreau or concentrated frozen orange juice
- 1/2 pint heavy cream
- 1 tablespoon powdered sugar
- 1 teaspoon vanilla

Reserve 4 pretty berries. Slice the others, place in a large bowl, and sprinkle with half the sugar. Slice the pineapple in half along its length. (Handle the leaves carefully to keep them intact.) With a curved grapefruit knife, slice under the fruit and empty the halves. Drain the juice (it won't be used). Remove the core from the pineapple pieces and discard it. Cut the fruit into chunks. Combine the chunks with the berries, the remaining sugar, and the Cointreau or orange juice concentrate. Whip the cream with the powdered sugar and vanilla until stiff. Scrape the fruit into the pineapple boats, cover with mounds of sweetened whipped cream, and chill in the freezer for 30 to 60 minutes before serving. Garnish with the reserved berries.

HONEYDEW BOATS STUFFED WITH RASPBERRIES

Preparation time: 10–20 minutes **Serves 4**

Cool and sophisticated, this is very, very nice after a rich dinner.

- 1 large honeydew melon, chilled
- 1 juicy lime, halved
- 1 pint raspberries
- 1 1/2 tablespoons sugar

Split and seed the melon, and divide it again, to make 4 wedges. Sprinkle each with the juice of half the lime. Divide the other lime half into 4 wedges. Rinse and drain the raspberries and set half of them to air-dry on paper towels. Shake the others free of water and puree them in a food processor, a blender, or by hand with the sugar. In a bowl, gently combine the whole berries and the puree, until all the berries are coated with raspberry sauce. Spoon the berries into the melon boats and garnish each with a wedge of lime.

Variations: Raspberries and Grapes in Melon Boats—Same procedure, but instead of using a pint of berries, combine 1 cup of small, seedless green grapes with half a pint of raspberries (1 cup) and the sugar—there is no berry puree.
Raspberries and Blueberries in Melon Boats—Use blueberries instead of the seedless grapes called for in the preceding recipe.
Strawberries and Raspberries in Melon Boats—Another variation that is bright and tasty: Halve 1 cup of hulled, rinsed strawberries and toss them with the raspberry puree made as directed with 1 cup (or 1/2 pint) of raspberries and sugar. Complete the recipe with lime wedges.

STRAWBERRY-MANGO CREAM WITH SAFFRON

Preparation and chilling time: 1 hour **Serves 6–8**

This is one of our favorite hurry-up desserts. The saffron gives it an exotic flavor that goes beautifully with mangoes and berries.

- 1 pint vanilla yogurt
- 1 pint sour cream
- 1/4 cup sugar
- 1/8 teaspoon saffron threads
- 1 pint strawberries
- 1 ripe chilled mango
- 1 teaspoon grated orange rind (optional)

In a large serving bowl, combine the yogurt, sour cream, sugar, and saffron. Slice rinsed, hulled, air-dried berries into the cream. Peel and slice the mango into bite-size chunks and mix in. Sprinkle orange rind, if you wish, over the cream. Chill before serving.

BANANA CUP PAÏNEY

Preparation and chilling time: 40 minutes **Serves 4**

Bananas with lemon juice and sugar make a perfect sweet-sour background for berries. Ripe bananas are a rich yellow flecked with brown.

- 4 ripe bananas
- Juice of 1/2 lemon
- 4–8 teaspoons brown sugar
- 1 pint strawberries
- 1/2 pint heavy cream

Slice peeled bananas into four dessert cups and sprinkle with lemon juice and sugar, 1 to 2 teaspoons to each cup. Top the bananas with rinsed, hulled, sliced berries and cream. Chill until ready to serve.

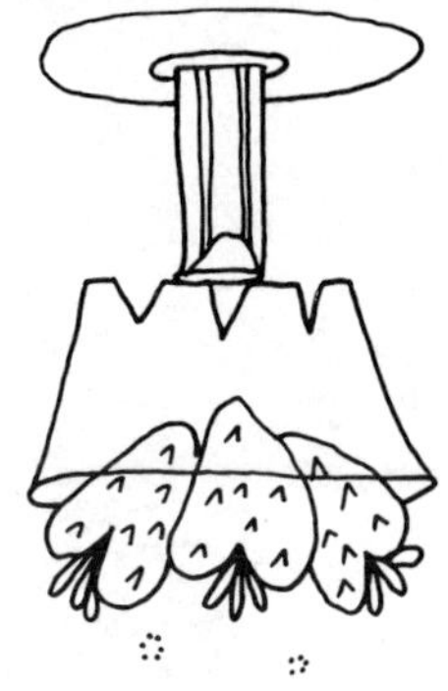

STRAWBERRIES WILHELMINA

Preparation time: 15 minutes
Chilling time: 30 minutes–2 hours or more **Serves 4**

A sharp hint of cherries comes from the liqueur and makes an exquisite contrast with the whipped cream. Grand Marnier is a good variation on Kirsch. Be aware that liqueurs and wines that have been cooked in a recipe lose their alcohol content, but uncooked liqueurs and wines used with fruit do not.

- 1 1/2 pints strawberries
- 1/3 cup extrafine or granulated sugar
- 3 tablespoons Kirsch
- 1 1/2 pints heavy cream
- 2 tablespoons sugar
- 1/2 teaspoon vanilla

Rinse and hull the strawberries, and air-dry them. Reserve 4 fine berries for a garnish. Slice the rest and layer in a glass bowl. Sprinkle each layer of berry slices with sugar and a few drops of Kirsch. Cover and chill for 30 minutes to 2 hours or more. Just before serving, whip the cream with 2 tablespoons sugar and the vanilla, and serve with the berries.

Variations: Strawberries in Champagne—Select a fruity champagne, such as Asti Spumante. Prepareberries as for the recipe above, sprinkle with 1 or 2 tablespoons of sugar and 1/2 cup champagne. Chill for 2 or 3 hours before serving. (By "champagne" I mean a sparkling wine—bubbly.)

Strawberries in Wine—Follow the instructions for Strawberries in Champagne, but sprinkle with 1/3 cup of sugar and 1/2 cup of a mellow but light red wine or a fruity white such as May wine, Liebfraumilch, or any of the Moselles, such as Ockfener Bockstein.

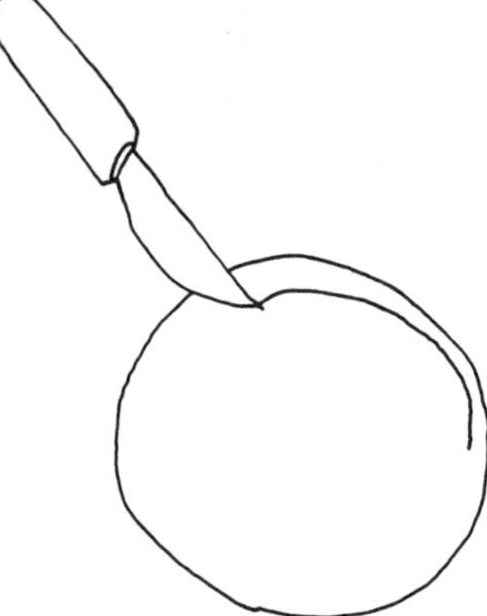

ORANGE CUP WITH BERRIES

Preparation time: 10 minutes **Serves 4**

This is on our cover—it is pretty and easy to make. Children love the gala of cut-out orange cups and the hint of orange in their berries.

- 1 pint raspberries
- 2 tablespoons sugar
- 4 big eating oranges
- 1/2 pint heavy cream
- 1 tablespoon sugar

Put the berries in a large bowl and sprinkle with 2 tablespoons sugar.

With a small, sharp knife, cut a pair of deep parallel lines to make a handle across the top half of an orange. (See the illustration at left and think the moves through before you cut.)

Draw a serrated outline halfway down the orange on either side of the handle with a pen. With the knife, cut through the rind and into the orange flesh just above the tops of the serrated marks on either side of the orange. Pull away the rind between the handle edges and the lines you have just cut, and scoop out all the orange flesh. With the knife, cut away the rind along the serrated outlines.

Cut the orange flesh into small pieces and combine with the berries. Complete all the oranges, using about half the orange flesh to add to the berries in the bowl, then spoon the berry-orange mixture into the orange cups, and chill. Serve with heavy cream whipped until thickened with 1 tablespoon sugar.

Variation: Grapefruit Cups with Fruit—Small grapefruits make pretty cups, and hold more fruit than the orange cups. The cups are bitter on occasion, so sprinkle the interiors with sugar before you put in the fruit, just enough sugar to add a hint of sweet.

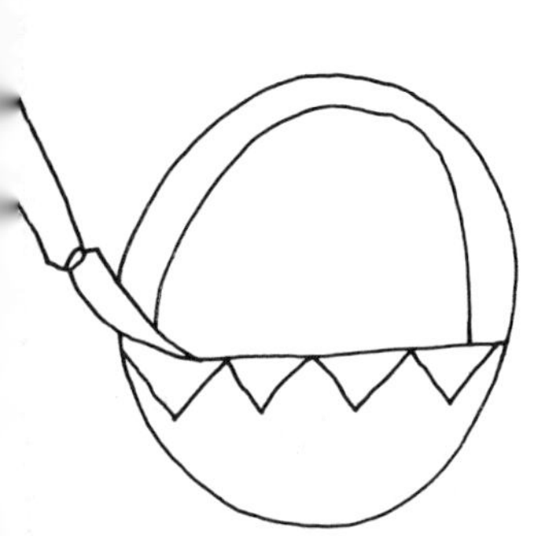

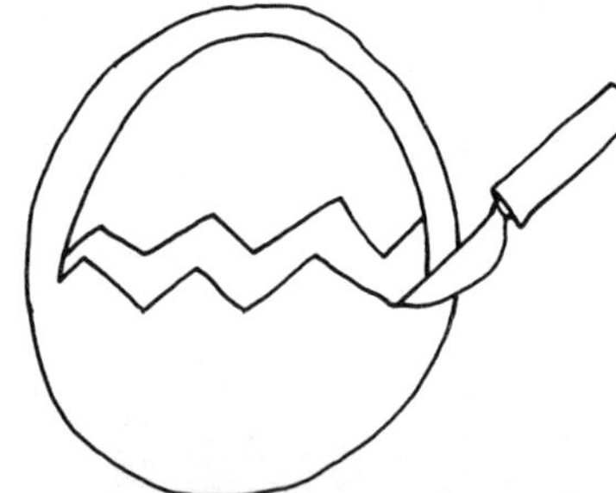

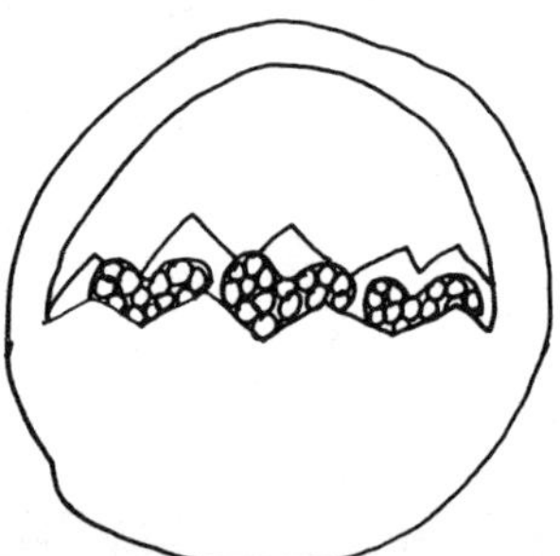

TROPICAL FRUIT PLATE

Preparation time: 15 minutes **Serves 4**

This takes only a few minutes to put together. It's my favorite hot day luncheon. Choose gold-green grapes—they are usually sweeter than green-green grapes, which often are rather tasteless.

- 1 small bunch seedless green grapes
- 1 pink grapefruit
- 1 good eating orange
- 1 large ripe mango
- 2 ripe bananas
- 1/2 pint strawberries
- 1/4 pint raspberries
- 1 kiwi fruit
- 8 ounces large-curd cottage cheese
- 1/2 pint sour cream

Pick and rinse the grapes; drain and air-dry them. Peel the grapefruit, orange, and mango, and cut the citrus fruits into 4 pieces. Cut the mango into 8 slices. Peel the bananas. Set out four plates and on each arrange one slice each of grapefruit and orange and two of mango. Slice the bananas thickly and arrange in little heaps in the center of each plate. Rinse, air-dry, and divide the strawberries and raspberries among the plates (don't hull the strawberries), putting them together in little piles. Peel the kiwi fruit, slice into four rings, and stand among the strawberries and raspberries. Tuck a dollop of cottage cheese among the heaps on each plate, and put another of sour cream beside it. Scatter grapes over the fruits; chill.

Variation: Tropical Fruit in a Watermelon—This makes a gala dessert for buffets, and will serve 12. Omit the cottage cheese and sour cream. Double the fruits in the recipe above, and add finger fruits—such as tiny bunches of grapes, cherries (about a pound), small fresh figs (a dozen), red bananas, peeled, dredged in lemon juice, and cut into thick chunks, 2 or 3 papayas, peeled and cut into wedges. Carve the top half of the watermelon away, as described on page 20 for the Orange Cup, to create a handle. Scoop out the watermelon meat, seed it, cut into big chunks, and fill the melon with these and the other fruits. Sprinkle with lemon juice and a liqueur to enhance the flavor, and chill for an hour before serving.

STRAWBERRY AND YOGURT SOUP

Preparation time: 15–20 minutes
Chilling time: 4 hours–overnight

Serves 6

This is an icy fruit soup to serve at a summer luncheon, as they do in Sweden, with hot biscuits and a tender salad (Boston or Bibb lettuce, for instance) seasoned with a light dressing and dill. It can be made from 2 pints of frozen strawberries.

- 2 pints strawberries
- 1/2 cup sugar
- 1 cup water
- 2 teaspoons lemon juice
- 1 1/2 pints plain yogurt
- 1 pint heavy cream
- Sugar
- Fresh mint sprigs (optional)

Reserve 6 pretty red berries. Rinse and hull the rest and puree them in a blender or a food processor or mash by hand.

In a large saucepan over medium-high heat, simmer the sugar, water, and lemon juice for 10 minutes. Let cool. Stir the pureed berries into the syrup. Combine the yogurt and cream, and fold in. Add sugar to taste. Cover and chill anywhere from 4 hours to overnight. Just before serving, add the reserved berries and a garnish of mint sprigs, if you wish.

RASPBERRY–ORANGE SOUP

Preparation time: 15–20 minutes
Chilling time: 4 hours–overnight **Serves 6**

A wonderfully intense raspberry experience! This also may be made from a pint of frozen raspberries and their juices.

- 3 cups water
- 1 stick cinnamon
- 2 whole cloves
- 1/4 cup lemon juice
- 2 tablespoons cornstarch
- 2 tablespoons cold water
- 3 tablespoons sugar
- 1 tablespoon butter
- Pinch of salt
- 1 teaspoon grated orange rind
- 1 pint raspberries, mashed
- 1 12-ounce can frozen orange juice concentrate
- 1 cup heavy cream, whipped and sweetened

In a kettle over medium-high heat, combine the water, cinnamon, cloves, and lemon juice. Bring to a boil, cover, lower the heat, and simmer for 5 minutes. Discard the cinnamon stick and cloves; reduce the heat.

In a small bowl, combine the cornstarch and cold water and stir them into the hot broth with the sugar. Cook until the mixture thickens and clears—2 to 3 minutes. Stir in the butter, salt, orange rind, and mashed berries. Cook for 2 or 3 minutes. Pour into a serving bowl and mash the orange juice concentrate into the berry mixture. Cover and chill anywhere from 4 hours to overnight. Just before serving, garnish with dollops of whipped cream.

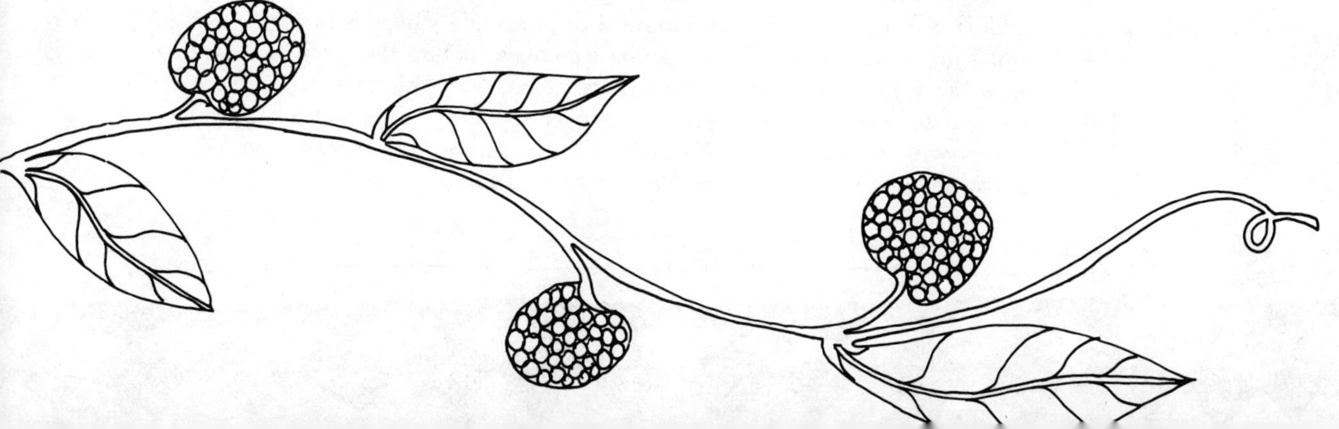

THE ICE CREAM PARLOR

BANANA SPLIT

Preparation time: 15 minutes **Serves 4**

In the 30s, boys proved their love by treating a girl to a banana split! You really need a horizontal sundae dish to set this out properly, but I use a half-moon glass salad plate. Use homemade ice cream, page 30, and jam, page 61—and wow! What a treat!

- 24 ounces good bittersweet chocolate
- 1/2 pint heavy cream
- 2 tablespoons sugar
- 4 large ripe bananas
- 4 scoops vanilla ice cream
- 4 scoops strawberry ice cream
- 4 scoops chocolate ice cream
- 4 tablespoons pineapple jam, or Strawberry and Pineapple Jam (p. 61)
- 1 cup berry sauce (pp. 12, 13, or 51)
- 4 tablespoons marshmallow sauce (optional)
- 1/2 cup chopped walnuts or pecans
- 4 maraschino cherries

Set the chocolate to melt in a small double boiler over simmering water, and whip the heavy cream with the sugar until stiff.

Set out four big dessert plates and peel, halve, and split the bananas to make 16 pieces. Divide these among the plates, 4 pieces to each in pairs facing each other at either end of the plate. Place a scoop of vanilla ice cream between each right-hand pair of banana pieces; a scoop of strawberry ice cream between each left-hand pair of banana pieces; a scoop of chocolate ice cream in the middle of the plate. Scrape a spoonful of pineapple jam or Strawberry and Pineapple Jam over each scoop of vanilla ice cream; dollop the strawberry ice cream with berry sauce; load the chocolate ice cream with the melted chocolate. Dribble marshmallow sauce, if you wish, over the other three sauces. Sprinkle the sauces with chopped nuts. Garnish, using a pastry tube if you have one, with the sweetened whipped cream. Set a cherry on top.

STRAWBERRY SUNDAE

Preparation time: 10 minutes **Serves 4**

Do you remember the thrill of realizing you could be your own ice cream parlor? I think we discovered this when I was about nine, and I have never quite gotten over it. To make sundaes for 4, you'll need a quart of each ice cream, though you may not use all of it.

- 1 cup Strawberry Sauce (p. 13)
- 4 tablespoons pineapple jam, or conserve
- 4 scoops strawberry ice cream
- 4 scoops vanilla ice cream
- 1/2 pint heavy cream
- 2 tablespoons sugar
- 1/2 teaspoon vanilla
- 1/4 cup chopped walnuts
- 4 strawberries

Prepare the sauce, and cool.

Divide the jam among four glass sundae or dessert dishes and add to each a scoop of strawberry and one of vanilla ice cream. Whip the cream with the sugar and the vanilla. Pour 1/4 cup of Strawberry Sauce over each, then a dollop of the whipped cream. Top with walnuts, and a berry for garnish. Serve at once.

RASPBERRY PARFAIT

Preparation time: 30–40 minutes
Chilling time: 2–4 hours
Serves 4–6

Raspberry parfait in a restaurant consists of layers of ice cream and liqueur. Here is an old-fashioned parfait: It demands effort, but it is delicious. This quantity fills four dessert cups or six flutes.

- 4 egg whites at room temperature
- 1/8 teaspoon cream of tartar
- Pinch of salt
- 1/2 cup sugar
- 1/2 cup water
- 1 pint raspberries
- 3 tablespoons sugar
- 1 tablespoon raspberry liqueur (optional)
- 1 pint heavy cream
- 1 teaspoon sugar
- Cointreau or Grand Marnier (optional)
- 4 mint sprigs (optional)

In a large bowl, beat the egg whites with the cream of tartar and salt until stiff.

In a small saucepan over medium heat, combine the sugar and water and simmer without stirring until the syrup spins a thread. (Keep dipping a fork into the syrup as it cooks and watch the drops fall back into the pot. In about 8 to 10 minutes, the syrup will boil down and the drops will become slow to fall. Soon after, a very fine thread will spin out as a drop falls. Remove the syrup from the heat at once.) Very slowly, dribble by dribble, beat the syrup into the whites. Beat until the whites are cool, then put the bowl in the freezer.

Rinse, drain, and air-dry the berries. Reserve 8 and puree the rest in a food processor, a blender, or by hand with the 3 tablespoons of sugar and the liqueur, if desired.

Whip the heavy cream until it is stiff but not dry. Take the egg white mixture from the freezer and fold into it the whipped cream, reserving 1/2 cup whipped cream. Fold in the berry puree, reserving 1/4 cup puree. Divide the reserved purée among four glass dessert cups. Scrape a quarter of the egg-white-cream mixture into each cup. Stir 1 teaspoon of sugar into the reserved whipped cream, divide among the parfaits, and top with the reserved berries. Cover with plastic wrap or foil and freeze for 2 to 4 hours. If you wish, add a teaspoon or two of liqueur to each dessert and garnish with mint sprigs before serving.

LEMON-RASPBERRY SHERBET

Preparation time: 30–40 minutes
Processing and freezing time: 4–6 hours **Serves 6**

This is a wonderful tart sherbet to complement a rich meal or a summer luncheon. I made it in the freezer before I acquired ice-cream-making equipment. The graininess of desserts made this way does a disservice to ice cream, but not to sherbets and frozen ices. If you wish to make this in the freezer, put it in a bowl, take the bowl out several times during the freezing process, and beat the mixture long enough to break up the crystals of ice that are forming.

2 pints raspberries
Grated rind of 1/2 orange
1/2 cup granulated sugar
2 1/2 cups cold water
1/2 cup milk
1/4 cup Cointreau

Rinse, drain, and air-dry the berries. Puree them in a food processor, a blender, or by hand. Toss with the grated rind and set aside.

Combine the sugar and water in a medium-size saucepan and bring to a simmer over medium heat. Simmer uncovered, without stirring, until the syrup spins a thread (see the instructions for this on p. 26). Whip the syrup into the fruit, and blend in the milk and liqueur. Turn into an ice-cream-maker bowl and follow the manufacturer's instructions.

ICE-CREAM-MAKING EQUIPMENT

Today's ice-cream-making equipment is creating a dessert revolution. I haven't yet revved up enough to acquire a Magic Chef Refrigerator à la Mode, which, I understand, has built-in "stir-freezing" equipment to make ice cream. But I use and love my little electric model, which produces good ice cream, frozen yogurt, and sherbets. Before you commit pints of expensive berries to an ice-cream maker, familiarize yourself with the manufacturer's instructions. Make some simple ice creams. Then you can move quickly and comfortably through the recipes that follow. They should work with any good brand of ice-cream and frozen-dessert equipment. A suggestion: if your equipment requires the use of rock salt, ask your hardware store for it. It is much less expensive than the fine salt sold in grocery stores—though that can be used instead.

FROZEN STRAWBERRY YOGURT

Preparation and processing time: 1–1 1/2 hours **Serves 4**

- 1 pint strawberries
- 1 envelope unflavored gelatin
- 1 cup sugar
- 1/4 teaspoon salt
- 1 tablespoon lemon juice
- 24 ounces plain yogurt

Rinse, hull, and puree the berries in a food processor, a blender, or by hand. In a small heavy saucepan over medium heat, combine half the berry puree with the gelatin and stir until the gelatin has dissolved completely. Stir in the sugar and salt, and continue to stir until the sugar has dissolved. Pour the hot mixture into the bowl containing the remaining puree and add the lemon juice, stirring constantly. Chill thoroughly in the freezer, about 1 hour.

Pour the yogurt into a large bowl and stir into it the chilled puree. Scrape the mixture into the container of an ice-cream maker, and follow manufacturer's instructions for processing.

FROZEN RASPBERRY YOGURT

Preparation and processing time: 1–1 1/2 hours **Serves 4**

This is richer and creamier than the Frozen Strawberry Yogurt recipe.

1/2 pint raspberries
1/2 cup evaporated milk
1/2 cup sugar
Pinch of salt
1 envelope unflavored gelatin, softened in 1/4 cup water
20 ounces plain yogurt
1/4 cup heavy cream

Rinse, drain, and puree the berries in a food processor, a blender, or by hand. Strain the berry juice into a small, heavy saucepan and reserve the fruit. Stir the milk, sugar, salt, and the gelatin into the juice. Set over low heat and stir until the gelatin has dissolved completely. Remove from the heat, scrape into a cold metal bowl, and chill thoroughly in the freezer, about 1 hour.

Pour the yogurt into a large bowl, and stir into it the cream, the gelatin mixture, and reserved fruit. Scrape the mixture into the container of an ice-cream maker and follow manufacturer's instructions for processing.

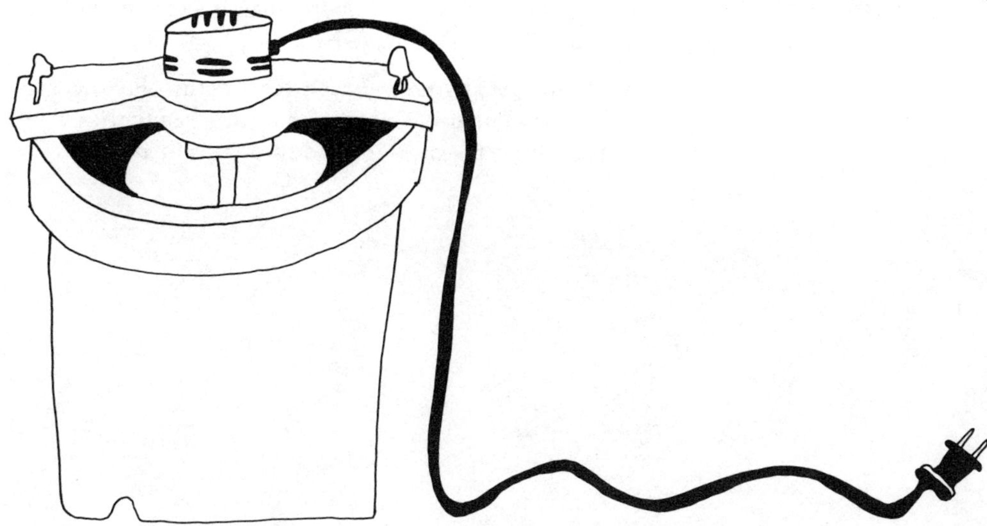

STRAWBERRY ICE CREAM

Preparation time: about 1 1/2 hours **Serves 12–16**

This is old-fashioned ice cream, made from a custard you cook before adding the fruit. The strawberries must be fully ripe and richly flavored. It is loaded with cream—umm! One pint of berries yields between 1 and 1 1/2 cups of halved berries—to get 4 cups halved berries you need about 3 pints of berries.

- 5 large eggs
- 1 1/2 cups granulated sugar
- 1/8 teaspoon salt
- 2 cups milk, scalded
- 4 cups heavy cream, scalded
- 4 cups halved strawberries
- 1 tablespoon strained lemon juice
- 1 teaspoon vanilla
- 3 drops red food coloring

In a large bowl with an electric beater, beat the eggs until thick, and, still beating, dribble in the sugar and add the salt. Fold in the milk and cream, then pour into a large heavy saucepan and stir over low heat until the custard thickens and coats the spoon. Set in the freezer and chill well, about 1 hour.

Combine the berries with the lemon juice. Stir the vanilla into the chilled custard, then fold in the berries and their juices and red food coloring. Process in an ice-cream maker, following manufacturer's instructions. Store in the freezer in a large plastic tub, covered.

Variation: Strawberry-Peach Ice Cream—Follow the basic recipe for Strawberry Ice Cream but use 3 cups of halved strawberries and 1 cup of very ripe, peeled, pitted, sliced peaches, instead of 4 cups of berries.

ICE CREAM TORTE

Preparation time: 40 minutes
Freezing time: 3 hours **Serves 8–10**

A nifty party dessert, much easier to make than it looks when finished.

- 1 recipe Pecan Shortcake Pie Crust (below)
- 1 recipe Raspberry or Strawberry Sauce (pp. 12, 13)
- 1/2 gallon vanilla ice cream
- 1/2 pint heavy cream
- 2 tablespoons sugar
- 4 ounces sweet chocolate bar, good quality

Prepare the pie crust and the berry sauce.

Spoon the berry sauce over the bottom of the crust and freeze for 1 hour. Meanwhile, let the ice cream soften to spreading consistency in the refrigerator. Take the pie crust from the freezer and quickly spoon ice cream over the bottom. Return to the freezer and freeze for 1 hour. Cover with dollops of the heavy cream that has been whipped stiff with the sugar. Return to the freezer for another hour. When ready to serve, use a potato peeler to scrape curls of chocolate over the pie. Serve at once.

PECAN SHORTCAKE PIE CRUST

Preparation time: 10 minutes **Yield: 1 nine-inch crust**

- 15–18 pecan shortcake biscuits, or "sandies"
- 1/3 cup sugar
- 1/4 cup butter, melted

In a food processor or a blender, crush the biscuits or "sandies" to crumbs. Blend in the sugar, then the butter. Turn the crumbs out onto a 9-inch pie plate and press together to make a crust. Press an 8-inch pie plate into it to compact the crumbs and shape the crust smoothly.

RASPBERRY YOGURT SHAKE

Preparation time: 5 minutes **Serves 2**

The tartness of plain yogurt brings out the flavor in very ripe raspberries, and together they make a great drink.

1 cup plain yogurt
1/2 cup milk
1 cup raspberries
3 thick ice cubes
2 tablespoons sugar or more

In a blender or food processor, combine all the ingredients and process until you don't hear the ice anymore. Taste; add sugar if needed.

RASPBERRY FLIP

Preparation time: 5 minutes **Serves 1**

1 scoop raspberry sherbet
1/2 cup coconut milk or whole milk
2 ice cubes

Put everything into a blender or food processor and process until the ice stops making noise. Serve the drink in a tall glass.

Variations: Strawberry Flip—Blend together 1 cup hulled strawberries, 1 cup of milk, 5 ice cubes, and sugar to taste. Serves 2.
Strawberry Soda Maison—In a 12-ounce or taller glass, place 2 scoops of hard-frozen strawberry ice cream, 1 heaping teaspoon of strawberry jam warmed enough to be runny (heat it briefly over a stove-top burner in a ladle), and either ginger ale or plain soda. It will froth wildly, and as it does, be ready to stir up the jam in the bottom with a long-handled sherbet spoon or a fork. Put two straws and the spoon into the glass, and *voilà*—Strawberry Soda Maison! Serves 1.

STRAWBERRY MILKSHAKE

Preparation time: 5 minutes **Serves 1**

- 1 cup coconut milk or whole milk
- 1 large scoop strawberry ice cream
- 1/2 cup very ripe strawberries, hulled

Pour the milk into the container of a blender or a food processor and add the ice cream. Cover and turn the motor to high for 15 seconds. Remove the cover and add the berries to the container while still processing; process for 1/2 minute. Serve in a 12-ounce glass.

STRAWBERRY-ORANGE FROST

Preparation time: 5 minutes **Serves 2**

- 1 cup orange juice
- 2 scoops vanilla ice cream
- 1 cup ripe strawberries, hulled

Pour the juice into the container of your blender or food processor, and add the ice cream. Cover, and turn the motor to high for 1/2 minute. Remove the cover and add the berries to the container while processing; process for 1/2 minute. Serve in tall glasses.

RASPBERRY-ORANGE BREAKFAST DRINK

Preparation time: 10 minutes **Serves 1**

- 1 juice orange
- 1/2 cup raspberries
- 1–2 tablespoons honey
- 1 cup milk
- 3 ice cubes

Peel and seed the orange and cut into chunks. Put all ingredients in the blender or food processor and process until you don't hear the cubes anymore. Pour into a tall glass.

BERRIES 'N' CREAM

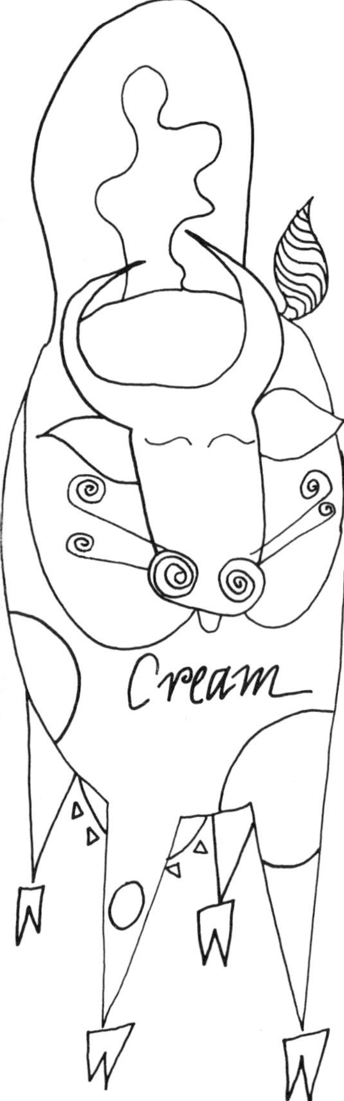

COEUR À LA CRÈME

Preparation time: 10 minutes
Setting time: overnight **Serves 6–8**

"Heart of cream" is what the name means, and it is the classic French dessert of berries and cream made in a heart-shape mold.

- 16 ounces cream cheese
- 16 ounces creamy large-curd cottage cheese
- 1/8 teaspoon salt
- 1 pint heavy cream
- 1 recipe Strawberry Sauce (p. 13)

In a food processor or with an electric beater, beat the cream cheese until it is soft. Beat in the cottage cheese and salt, and then with a whisk, mix in the heavy cream until completely combined. Wet a double thickness of cheesecloth and line the mold with it. Pack the cream mixture in the mold and smooth out the top. Cover with the ends of the cheesecloth and set in the refrigerator on a dish that will keep the bottom of the mold raised for easy draining. Chill overnight.

Prepare and chill the Strawberry Sauce, reserving a few berries for garnish. When ready to serve, unmold the cheese heart onto a flat serving dish, garnish with berries, and serve with Strawberry Sauce.

STRAWBERRY-RHUBARB MOUSSE

Preparation and cooling time: 40 minutes **Serves 4–6**

The ultimate sweet-and-sour berries-and-cream dessert.

- 4 cups rhubarb
- 1/3 cup sugar
- Pinch of salt
- 1 pint strawberries
- 1 pint heavy cream
- 1 tablespoon sugar

In a large kettle over medium heat, stir rhubarb, sugar, and salt until mixture begins to bubble. Simmer on low for 10 or 15 minutes more, until the rhubarb is just tender. Meanwhile, rinse, drain, and hull the berries and cut into small pieces. Whip the cream with the sugar until it is stiff. Transfer the cooked rhubarb to a serving bowl, combine with the berries, and chill in the freezer for 20 minutes. Fold the whipped cream into the fruit and refrigerate until ready to serve.

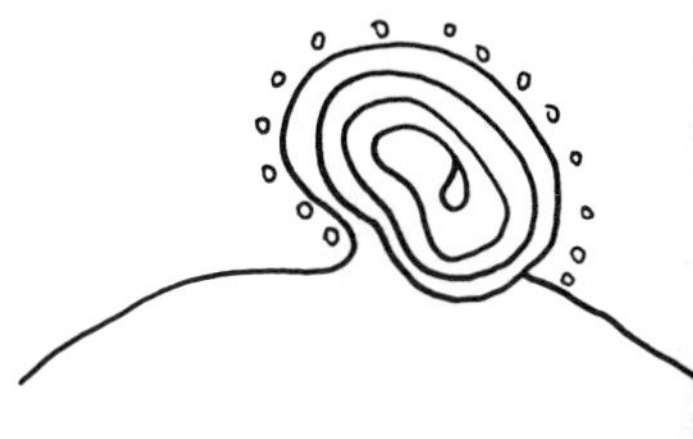

STRAWBERRY-ORANGE FOOL

Preparation time: 10–15 minutes
Chilling time: 1 hour or more

Serves 6–8

This recipe for a berry fool gives the basic proportions of cream, fruit, and sweet and fiery cordials that make a great dessert of almost any tart fruit, including oranges, mangoes, and many more. You can complete this hours ahead rather than at the last minute.

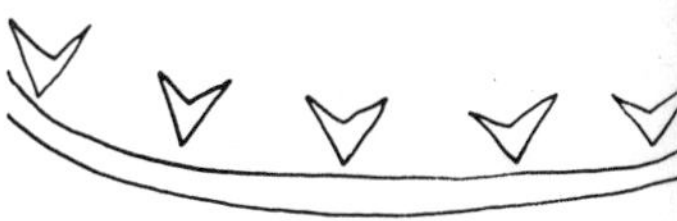

- 2 pints strawberries
- 1/4 cup sugar
- 1 teaspoon each of raspberry cordial, Cointreau, and strained lemon juice
- 1 pint heavy cream
- 1 tablespoon raspberry cordial
- 1 tablespoon Cointreau
- 1 tablespoon sugar
- 1 tablespoon grated orange rind

Rinse and drain the berries and puree them in a food processor, a blender, or by hand with the sugar and a teaspoonful of each of the cordials and the lemon juice. Allow to marinate at room temperature for an hour or so, then chill.

Just before serving, whip the cream with the remaining tablespoonfuls of cordials, sugar, and rind until stiff enough to peak, and turn into a serving bowl. Make a well in the center of the cream, pour the berry mixture into it, and with a large spoon, stir the berries gently around and around in the cream without completely mixing them.

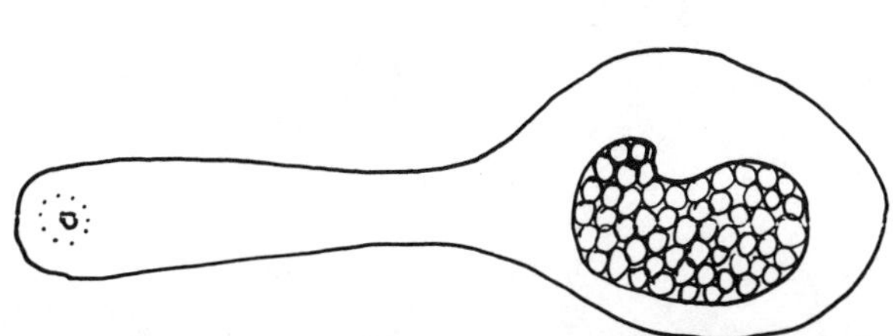

BAVARIAN CREAM WITH RASPBERRIES

Preparation time: 1 hour
Setting time: 4 hours–overnight

Serves 8–10

This is one of my favorites. My mother made it of canned pineapple chunks, but it is glorious made with raspberries.

1 1/2 pints raspberries
2 packages unflavored gelatin
1 1/2 cups milk
5 eggs
1 cup sugar
1 tablespoon lemon juice
1/2 teaspoon salt
1/4 teaspoon cream of tartar
1 cup heavy cream

Rinse, drain, and measure out 2 cups of the berries. Reserve the rest. Puree the 2 cups of berries in a food processor, a blender, or by hand, and strain, reserving 1 cup of juice and the pulp. Sprinkle the gelatin on the juice. Scald the milk. Separate the eggs and beat the yolks with the sugar until thick and lemon colored. Stir the hot milk into the yolks, return the mixture to a medium-size heavy saucepan, and stir over low heat, until custard forms and begins to coat the spoon. Turn off the heat and stir in the berry-juice-and-gelatin mixture. Stir in the lemon juice.

Beat the egg whites with the salt and cream of tartar until stiff peaks form. Fold the whites into the hot custard and pour into a serving dish. Chill in the freezer for 30 minutes.

Whip the heavy cream until stiff and fold into the chilled custard-berry mixture. Fold in the pureed fruit pulp and the reserved whole fruit.

Cover and chill for anywhere from 4 hours to overnight.

Variation: Charlotte with Fruit—Line the sides of a crystal serving bowl with ladyfingers, bottoms cut so they stand flat. Scoop the completed Bavarian Cream into the dish and chill anywhere from 4 hours to overnight. Garnish with reserved berries.

DOUBLE CREAM CHEESECAKE WITH STRAWBERRIES

Preparation time: 30–40 minutes
Baking time: 55 minutes **Serves 8–10**

This is the creamiest, richest cheesecake I know, the perfect foil for a sharp strawberry sauce. It is best chilled overnight.

- 14 double graham crackers
- 1/3 cup sugar
- 1/4 teaspoon vanilla
- 3/4 stick of butter, melted
- 2 16-ounce packages cream cheese
- 2 tablespoons heavy cream
- 3 large eggs, well beaten
- 1/2 cup sugar
- 1/4 teaspoon vanilla
- 1 pint sour cream
- 1/3 cup sugar
- 1/4 teaspoon vanilla
- 1 recipe Strawberry Sauce (p. 13)

Heat the oven to 325°.

In a large bowl, crush the crackers and stir in the 1/3 cup sugar, vanilla, and butter. Spread over the bottom of a 9-inch pie plate, and press an 8-inch pie plate into it to shape a crust. In a large bowl, with electric beaters, whip the cream cheese and the heavy cream until fluffy, then beat in the eggs, 1/2 cup sugar, and 1/4 teaspoon vanilla. Smooth the mixture into the crust and bake for 15 minutes. Raise the heat to 450° and bake for 15 minutes more. Remove and cool for 20 minutes. Turn the oven to 400°.

Mix the sour cream with the remaining 1/3 cup of sugar and 1/4 teaspoon of vanilla, and smooth over the cooled cheesecake top. Bake for 5 minutes. Cool for several hours. Serve with Strawberry Sauce.

Variation: Orange Cheesecake with Raspberry Sauce—Flavor the cream-cheese–egg mixture with 1/2 teaspoon lemon extract and 1 tablespoon grated orange rind, and omit the vanilla from this part of the recipe. Follow the recipe in other particulars, and serve with Raspberry Sauce, page 12.

JELLY ROLL SPONGE CAKE

Preparation and baking time: 35–40 minutes
Cooling time: 25 minutes **Serves 8–10**

This is a wonderfully light sponge cake, perfect to make jelly rolls and Bûche de Noël.

- 4 large eggs
- 2 tablespoons soft butter
- 1/4 teaspoon salt
- 1/4 teaspoon cream of tartar
- 3/4 cup sugar
- 1 teaspoon lemon flavoring
- 1 teaspoon grated orange rind
- 3/4 cup sifted cake flour
- 3/4 teaspoon baking powder

Put the eggs in a large bowl filled with hot water. Set the oven at 400°.

Butter the bottom and sides of a 15 1/2″ x 10 1/2″ x 1″ jelly roll pan. Cut a sheet of wax paper to fit exactly the bottom and sides of the jelly roll pan. Tuck it into the pan and butter the side facing you.

Take the eggs from the bowl, empty and dry the bowl, and break the eggs into it. Add the salt and cream of tartar. With the electric beaters on high, beat the eggs until they are thick and lemon colored. Beat the sugar into the eggs a teaspoon at a time, then the lemon flavoring and orange rind. Measure the sifted flour and the baking powder into a sifter and sift over the egg mixture, beating after each addition. Pour the batter into the jelly roll pan and smooth the top. Bake 13 to 15 minutes, then test. When done, the cake will be golden and will spring back if pressed gently. Remove from the oven to a rack.

Wet and completely ring out a clean dishtowel. Smooth the towel down on the counter. With a sharp knife, loosen the edges of the cake wherever it is stuck to the pan, and turn the pan upside down over the towel. If it sticks, tug down on an edge of the paper or press a flexible metal spatula between the paper and the pan and push down until the cake falls. Peel the paper away from the cake and, with scissors, snip off the crisped edges on the long sides. Roll the cake and towel up together gently from the narrow end, and return to the rack to complete cooling—25 minutes or more.

Unroll the cake and spread with fruit sauce or jam sauce. Roll the cake up again, and use the towel to flip it onto a serving plate.

RASPBERRY-ORANGE ROLL WITH TWO SAUCES

Preparation and baking time: 35–40 minutes
Cooling time: 25 minutes **Serves 8–10**

The airy sponge cake base makes this very rich dessert light as a feather. It's a great cake for early summer parties, when both berries are in season. You must have a jelly roll pan and wax paper to make it. I've tried it with oiled supermarket brown bags instead of wax paper, and the cake stuck adamantly to the paper and was ruined.

- 1/2 recipe Strawberry Butter Sauce (p. 51)
- 1 recipe Raspberry Sauce (p. 12)
- 1 recipe Jelly Roll Sponge Cake (p. 38)
- 1 pint heavy cream
- 1 tablespoon sugar
- 1 teaspoon vanilla
- 6 raspberries for garnish
- 1 teaspoon grated orange rind

Prepare the two sauces and set the Strawberry Butter Sauce to cool. Make the Jelly Roll Sponge Cake, complete through cooling it wrapped in a damp dishtowel. Unroll the cake and spread with Raspberry Sauce. Roll the cake up again without the towel, and use the towel to flip the cake up over the edge of a large serving platter. Whip the cream with the sugar and the vanilla until stiff. Chill until ready to serve. Frost the cake with the whipped cream, garnish with raspberries and grated orange rind, and bring to the table with Strawberry Butter Sauce just warm enough to be runny. Cut a 1-inch slice across the cake with a sharp knife, flip over onto a pie server, and set on a dessert plate.

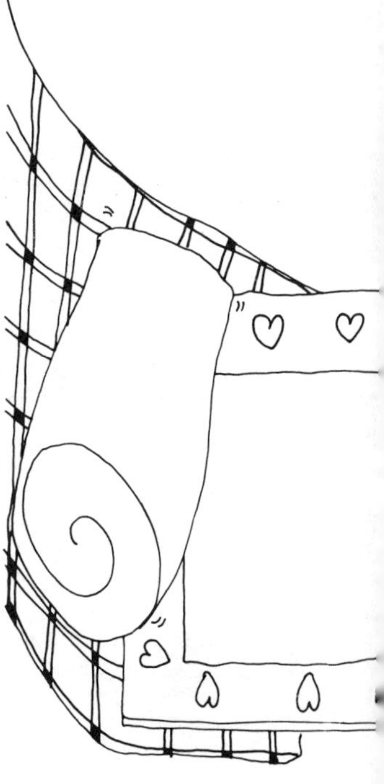

STRAWBERRY SHORTCAKES

Preparation and assembly time: 30–40 minutes **Serves 8–10**

Use different "cakes" to make berry shortcakes, depending on the ingredients in the meal. When the shortcake is to top a very light meal, use an enriched biscuit, the "shortcake" that gives the dessert its name. To be perfect, this must be made the minute before serving, so when I'm cooking ahead, I use instead my father's sponge cake or an angel-food cake mix, as in the Raspberry Angel Cake recipe, page 42. (I've made angel-food cake from scratch and didn't find it better than the mix.)

- 2 pints strawberries
- 1/2 cup sugar
- 1 pint heavy cream
- 1 tablespoon sugar
- 1 teaspoon vanilla
- 1 recipe Shortcake Biscuits (p. 41), Marcel's Layer Cake (p. 43), or angel-food cake mix, baked

Three or four hours before you plan to serve dessert, hull and rinse the berries, and in a food processor or a blender, puree half the berries, including the least perfect berries, particularly the greenish and overly ripe ones. Reserve 5 or 6 perfect berries, quarter the rest and add to the puree. Stir in the 1/2 cup sugar, and leave at room temperature until you are ready to assemble the dessert. Whip the cream with the 1 tablespoon sugar and vanilla until almost stiff, turn into a serving bowl or pitcher, cover and chill. Prepare the cake base and allow to cool if using angel-food cake mix or Marcel's Layer Cake.

If you are using shortcakes, bake the cakes just before you sit down to the meal. This allows them a few minutes to cool. When you are ready to assemble the dessert, place the bottom half of the biscuits or cake on a serving dish, ladle a third of the berry sauce over it, cover with the top half, and ladle another third of the sauce over that. Put a dollop of whipped cream in the middle and garnish with the reserved berries. Bring to the table with the remaining third of the berry sauce and the cream, and add sauce and cream as you serve.

SHORTCAKE BISCUITS

Preparation and baking time: 25–30 minutes **Serves 8–10**

You can also make biscuits from biscuit mix: Add 2 tablespoons of sugar and 2 of butter to the mix and bake as directed.

- 2 cups all-purpose flour
- 1 tablespoon baking powder
- 1/4 teaspoon salt
- 2 tablespoons sugar
- 7 tablespoons cold butter
- 3/4–1 cup milk
- Flour
- Soft butter

Heat the oven to 450°.

In a food processor or a large mixing bowl, combine the dry ingredients and cut in the butter until the flour mixture is mealy. Pour into a large mixing bowl if you have been using the processor. Make a well in the center of the flour and stir in 3/4 cup milk and as much more as it takes to make a soft but not runny dough. Let the dough rest while you are preparing the berries and cream for shortcake.

Turn the dough onto a well-floured board, divide into two rounds, and pat out each round to about 1/2-inch thick. Slide the rounds around on the floured board to make sure they aren't sticking; if they are, spread around more flour, turn the dough rounds over and slide them around on the flour. Divide each round into 8 or 10 circles, using a cookie cutter or a glass turned upside down and dipped in flour. Or divide into squares, using a knife. Brush soft butter over each circle or square of one dough round. Lift these and place the floured bottoms on an ungreased cookie sheet. Cover each with a circle or square from the other round. Place the cookie sheet in the upper third of the oven and bake for 15 to 20 minutes, or until the biscuits are golden brown. Remove the cookie sheet from the oven and allow the biscuits to cool for about 5 minutes.

Place each biscuit in an individual soup plate, or put all the biscuits on a large serving plate. Lift the top half of each biscuit off and let it cool before putting a little butter on the bottom half. Then proceed with crushed berries and whipped cream as described on page 40.

RASPBERRY ANGEL CAKE

Preparation time: 2 hours **Serves 8–10**

"Real" (or old-fashioned) strawberry shortcakes are made with fresh, hot biscuits. For raspberries, I do something more ethereal. It's easy.

- 1 box angel-food cake mix
- 2 pints raspberries
- 6 tablespoons sugar
- 1 pint heavy cream
- 2 tablespoons sugar
- 1 teaspoon vanilla

Mix and bake the angel-food cake, following package instructions.

While the cake is baking, rinse and air-dry the berries. Set aside 1/4 cup of fine berries; combine half the remaining berries with half the sugar and toss gently. Set aside. In a food processor or a blender, combine the remaining berries and sugar, and puree. Pour into a small pitcher and chill.

Shortly before serving, whip the cream with the 2 tablespoons of sugar and vanilla until stiff. With two forks, break the angel cake into two layers or slice it very gently with a bread knife or a very sharp knife. Spread half the whipped cream on the bottom layer, and sprinkle the sugared whole berries over it. Cover with the top cake layer. Dollop the cream over the top layer and push until the cream begins to slide down the sides. Garnish with the 1/4 cup of whole berries and serve with the berry puree. Use a very sharp knife to cut the slices, sawing back and forth gently.

Variation: Berry Topping—Beat together 4 tablespoons each of soft butter and cream cheese with 1 cup of confectioners sugar, then beat in as many sliced raspberries or strawberries as the icing will absorb without becoming so runny it won't frost the cake.

MARCEL'S LAYER CAKE

Preparation and baking time: 50–60 minutes **Serves 10–12**

This is my chef father's favorite all-purpose sponge cake. He uses it as a base for his version of Strawberry Shortcakes because it is lighter than enriched biscuits and keeps and freezes well, so the dessert can be prepared in advance. When using Marcel's Layer Cake as a base for strawberry shortcake, increase the berries in the recipe on page 40 to 3 pints and the heavy cream to 1 1/2 pints. Add another 2 tablespoons of sugar to the berry sauce and increase the sugar for the whipped cream to 1 1/2 tablespoons. Add a few more drops of vanilla flavoring to the cream, too.

- 3 cups sifted cake flour
- 1 tablespoon baking powder
- 1/8 teaspoon salt
- 1 cup shortening
- 2 cups sugar
- 4 medium eggs
- 1 cup milk
- 1 teaspoon vanilla, almond, or other flavoring extract

Heat the oven to 375°.

Measure the flour, baking powder, and salt into a sifter and sift into a large bowl, three times.

In another large bowl, with an electric beater, cream the shortening with the sugar until fluffy. Add the eggs one at a time, beating well after each addition. Then add the flour mixture alternately with the milk in thirds, beating smooth after each addition. Add the extract, and blend. Pour batter into two buttered and floured 8″ by 8″ by 2″ square or round cake tins and bake for 25 minutes or until a straw comes out clean. Cool on a rack.

Variation: Birthday Cake with Berries—Prepare a full recipe Marcel's Layer Cake. Cool and cover the bottom layer with 1/2 recipe Crème Patissière Dumas, page 47. Cover the Crème with 2/3 pint of strawberries that have been hulled, rinsed, drained, sliced, and tossed with 2 tablespoons sugar. Set the second cake layer on top. Ice with Berry Topping, page 42, and garnish with the remaining 1/3 pint of berries. Use these berries as holders for birthday candles.

STRAWBERRY-RHUBARB PIE

Preparation time: 20 minutes
Baking time: 35–45 minutes **Serves 8**

A glorious sweet-sour combination, rhubarb and strawberries are a popular pair, just right with the addition of 3/4 cup sugar when the berries are garden ripened and very sweet. To trim rhubarb, cut away the leaf with about an inch of stalk, and shave away the tough portion at the other end.

- 3/4 pound rhubarb, trimmed and cut in 1-inch pieces
- 1 1/2 tablespoons cornstarch
- 1/2 lemon and rind
- 3/4–1 cup sugar
- 1/8 teaspoon salt
- 2 pints strawberries
- 1 recipe Flaky Pastry (p. 49) or prepared mix for a 2-crust pie
- 1 tablespoon butter
- 1/2 cup milk
- 1/2 pint heavy cream, whipped

In a large mixing bowl, combine the rhubarb with the cornstarch. Grate the lemon rind over them, add 1 tablespoon of lemon juice, the sugar and salt, and toss. Rinse, drain, and hull the berries, reserving a few.

Heat the oven to 425°.

Prepare the pie dough on a well-floured board, roll out 3/5 of the dough to make the bottom crust, and set it into a 2-inch-deep 9-inch pie plate or quiche dish. Toss half the berries with the rhubarb and put in the pie plate or quiche dish. Dot with the butter. Slice the remaining berries over the fruit, but not the reserved berries.

Roll out the remaining dough. Put the milk into a soup plate. Cut the dough into 1-inch-wide strips. Pick up a strip and twist the ends in opposite directions. Holding it firmly, dip the strip into the milk, just moistening each side a little. The milk helps the dough to color nicely. Fix the strip across the center of the pie. Repeat, making a lattice of strips. Moisten a pastry brush or a scrap of paper towel in the milk and brush any pastry not already moistened with milk.

This pie usually drips, so line the bottom of the oven with foil to catch the liquid. Bake the pie for 35 to 45 minutes. Remove from the oven, poke the remaining berries into open spaces in the latticework, and serve warm with cold whipped cream.

SOUR CHERRY AND RASPBERRY COBBLER

Preparation and baking time: 1 1/2 hours **Serves 6–8**

A cobbler is a deep-dish fruit pie with a topping made sometimes of pie dough, sometimes of biscuit batter, as here. It is a handy dessert because it is less messy and lots easier to make than a rolled-out pie. Delicious served with ice cream as well as whipped cream.

- Butter
- 1 pint raspberries
- 1 pound sour cherries, pitted
- 2/3 cup sugar
- 1 cup all-purpose flour
- 2 teaspoons baking powder
- 1 cup sugar
- 2 medium eggs, well beaten
- 1/4 cup milk
- 1 teaspoon vanilla
- 1 teaspoon grated orange rind
- 1 1/2 cups heavy cream
- 2 tablespoons confectioners sugar

Heat the oven to 350°. Butter a 2-quart mold, and in it toss the berries and cherries with the 2/3 cup sugar.

In a large bowl, sift the flour, baking powder, and 1 cup sugar together. Beat in the beaten eggs, milk, vanilla, and orange rind. Scrape over the berries and at once place in the preheated oven. Bake for 1 hour. Remove to a rack and allow to cool for 10 minutes. Serve with cream whipped medium thick with confectioners sugar.

STRAWBERRY CREAM PIE

Preparation time: 2 hours **Serves 8–10**

This is something to do on a rainy afternoon when you want to cook up a storm. t's the pie on the cover, one that is part of the great pastry repertoire of Madame Dumas of Dumas Pastry Shops in Manhattan (the best!). If you wish to duplicate it, make a shell of *pâte feuilletée*. This is French puff pastry which begins with a Flaky Pastry pie dough (p. 49) rolled out and spread with softened butter. The dough is folded over the butter, allowed to chill, then rolled out several times. It is a long, drawn-out process, and I think you'll have more fun working with the very quick and easy Pecan Shortcake Pie Crust I recommend. Which, by the way, is delicious for use with any pie or cheesecake.

- 1 recipe Pecan Shortcake Pie Crust (p. 31)
- 1/2 recipe Crème Patissière Dumas (p. 47)
- 3 pints big strawberries
- 1 8-ounce jar red currant jelly

Prepare the pie crust and smooth the Crème Patissière into the bottom. Select the 30 largest, reddest, most perfect berries. Rinse, hull, and air-dry them, and cut a thin slice from the bottoms so they will sit straight. Set them on a big cookie sheet, reserving the largest. Melt the jelly in the top of a small double boiler and keep it over the hot water, heat off. Brush the berries 3 or 4 at a time with the melted jelly and set them in a circle just inside the crust. Continue, filling toward the center. Set the largest berry in the middle. Chill until ready to serve.

CRÈME PATISSIÈRE DUMAS

Preparation and cooking time: 30 minutes Yield: filling for 2 pie shells

This is a baker's custard cream, used to fill cake layers and as a base in filled pie shells and tarts. Madame Dumas taught me to put whipped cream into it, which makes a much lighter crème patissière and the most delicious custard I've ever tasted. (I use leftovers to make custard cups for dessert, when I have leftovers.) The crème is easy to make; the trick is not to overheat the eggs, for they will curdle into scrambled eggs. I make the crème in a small, heavy saucepan of aluminum over very low heat, taking it off periodically if I suspect the pot is becoming too hot. Still, it has to have enough heat to thicken into custard within 10 or 15 minutes—so if yours is not thickening, increase the heat a little and stir quickly. Or make it over hot water in a small double boiler.

- 1 egg plus 3 egg yolks
- 3 tablespoons all-purpose flour
- 5 tablespoons sugar
- 1/2 cup hot milk
- 1 teaspoon vanilla
- 1/2 cup heavy cream

Break the whole egg and separate the yolks into a small bowl. Beat them at high speed with an electric beater for 1 minute. Put the flour and the sugar into a large bowl and use a whisk or a fork to whip the eggs smoothly into the mixture. Use a small heavy saucepan to heat the milk to simmering, and whip the milk into the batter. Pour the mixture back into the saucepan and, over low heat, with a whisk, cook and stir constantly until the sauce thickens to the consistency of thick mayonnaise. The whisk will leave tracks in the sauce when it is thick enough. Stir in the vanilla and allow to cool or chill in the freezer, but don't freeze. Stir a few times during the cooling to stop the formation of a skin on the custard.

Whip the cream and fold it into the custard. Use at once, or store covered in the refrigerator. It will keep three or four days.

RASPBERRY TARTS

Preparation and filling time: 2 hours **Serves 12**

This is the tartlet on the back cover. It's a labor of love for those to whom cooking is fun. Don't bother unless you can find perfect sweet, ripe raspberries and have lots of time. I suggest tart shells made from a regular pie dough, but the tartlet on the cover was made with a traditional tart pastry. To make traditional tart pastry, mound 2 cups of sifted all-purpose flour on a pastry board, make a well in the center, and in the well with your fingers, mix 5 tablespoons sugar, 4 large egg yolks, then with your fingers work in enough soft butter, in pieces, to make a soft dough. Then work in the outer portions of the flour to form a smooth, round ball. If the dough seems dry, add a few teaspoons of water. Knead, wrap in wax paper, and chill for an hour or so before rolling out and cutting to fit tart baking tins.

- 12 baked 3-inch Tart Shells (p. 49)
- 4 cups raspberries
- 6 tablespoons sugar
- 1/2 recipe Crème Patissière Dumas (p. 47)
- 1 8-ounce jar red currant jelly
- 1/4 cup pistachio nuts, chopped fine

Prepare and bake the tart shells; allow to cool. Reserve 1/4 of the berries, the best. Combine the remaining berries with the sugar, tossing gently in a large bowl. Line the bottom of each tart shell with a scant tablespoon of Crème Patissière, and over this spoon a portion of the berry-sugar mixture. Top with reserved berries, brush with currant jelly melted in a double boiler, and garnish with a scattering of chopped nuts.

FLAKY PASTRY

Preparation time: 20 minutes **Yield: 2 crusts**

2 cups all-purpose flour
1/2 teaspoon salt
2 teaspoons sugar
1/2 teaspoon baking powder
2/3 cup shortening
2 tablespoons cold butter
4 tablespoons ice water
Milk

Measure the flour, salt, sugar, and baking powder into a food processor or a large mixing bowl. If you are using a processor, mix the ingredients for a few seconds: if mixing by hand, sift the ingredients together once.

Cut the shortening into pieces into the flour, then cut in the butter. Process the mixture until it resembles coarse meal. If you are working by hand, use two knives to cut the shortening into the flour. Little by little, add the water to the flour-shortening mixture and stir until it forms a ball of dough. Divide the ball into two flat rounds, and let them rest for 20 to 30 minutes in a cool place. With a rolling pin on a well-floured board, roll the dough rounds to fit pie tins. After each roll, flip the dough a quarter turn. To move the rolled-out rounds, fold the dough in half, then in half again, and gently lift into an 8- or 9-inch pie plate. Fill, and cover with the remaining dough. Brush all over with milk and make a few slashes to let steam escape.

Variation: Tart Shells—Follow the basic recipe and complete to the rolling out of the dough. Cut rounds about 4 inches across, to fit into muffin tins with 3-inch cups. Butter the tins, gently tuck the cut-out pastry rounds into them, let rest for a few minutes, then shape the bottoms and sides to fit the tins. Into each, insert a foil muffin cup, bottom side buttered, and fill with rice or dried beans. Moisten the pastry tops with a little milk, and bake in an oven preheated to 425° for about 10 minutes. Remove the bean cups and turn the pastry cups upside down on a rack to cool completely. Set into paper or foil muffin cups in the baking tins and fill as directed. Yield is 8 tart shells.

BERRY BOUTIQUE

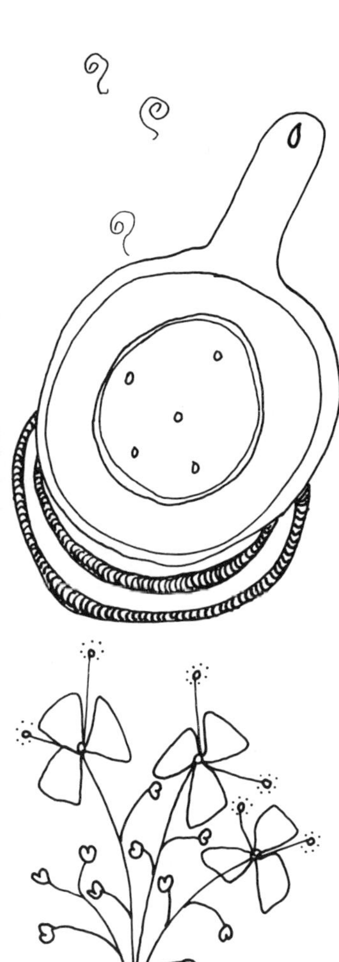

RASPBERRY PANCAKES WITH STRAWBERRY BUTTER SAUCE

Preparation time: 20–30 minutes **Serves 4–6**

This pancake recipe is great for raspberries or any other berry, and the Strawberry Butter Sauce is sheer heaven! This is our Sunday Brunch special. It's especially nice in May, during the first outdoor brunching days. Our friends like this with chilled May wine with a strawberry in it. Be prepared to be patient making the berry pancakes—they must be cooked at a lower heat than regular pancakes. The batter freezes well but will require additional milk to be the right consistency after thawing. The "right consistency" for berry pancakes is slightly runny, thinner than regular pancakes.

- 3 large eggs
- 1 cup milk
- 6 tablespoons melted butter
- 2 cups all-purpose flour
- 1 tablespoon baking powder
- 1 tablespoon sugar
- 1/2 teaspoon salt
- 1 pint raspberries, rinsed, air-dried
- Milk
- Butter
- 1 recipe hot Strawberry Butter Sauce (p. 51)

In a food processor or a large mixing bowl with an electric beater, beat the eggs, beat in the 1 cup milk, then the 6 tablespoons melted butter. Dribble in the flour, baking powder, sugar, and salt. If you have time, let the batter rest for 20 or 30 minutes, then gently fold in the berries. If the batter is very thick, add enough milk to make it runny.

Over medium heat, melt a little butter in a medium-size heavy pancake or crepe pan or skillet. When it is hot, pour in enough batter to make a pancake about 4 inches across. When bubbles have formed on the surface of the pancake—it takes about 5 to 6 minutes, be patient—and the batter begins to dry, flip the pancakes over with a spatula and cook for another 2 or 3 minutes on the other side. Lift onto a warm serving plate and set in a warming oven on low. Continue to make pancakes until all the batter is used; then serve with hot Strawberry Butter Sauce.

STRAWBERRY BUTTER SAUCE

Preparation time: 20 minutes **Serves 6–8**

This I am absolutely mad about! It is an adaptation of a recipe from *The Christian Science Monitor*. The original suggests this, chilled, for use as butter on breakfast or tea breads—banana breads, for instance. But it is so good hot, we use it all the berry season on our pancakes. If a little is left over (rare), we serve it on vanilla ice cream and fruit.

- 1 pint hulled strawberries
- 1 tablespoon sugar
- 1/2 cup honey
- 1 tablespoon lemon juice
- 1 stick butter

Hull and rinse the berries and puree them in a food processor or a blender, or crush them by hand, with the sugar. Turn into a heavy medium-size saucepan over medium heat, and stir in the honey and lemon juice. Bring to a boil, reduce the heat, and simmer, uncovered, for 10 minutes. Turn off the heat and stir in the butter until it is melted.

Variations: Crepes with Strawberry Butter Sauce—Make crepes (which are pancakes thinned with 1 cup more milk than regular batter), pile them up with wax paper between each, keep warm, then place 1 tablespoon cold sour cream in the center of each and roll up the crepes. Arrange them on a warm serving dish, and serve with hot Strawberry Butter Sauce.

Blueberries with Strawberry Butter Sauce—Rinse and drain the berries and divide among dessert glasses. Top each with a dollop of sour cream and spoon Strawberry Butter Sauce over the cream. Chill until ready to serve. One pint of blueberries will serve four.

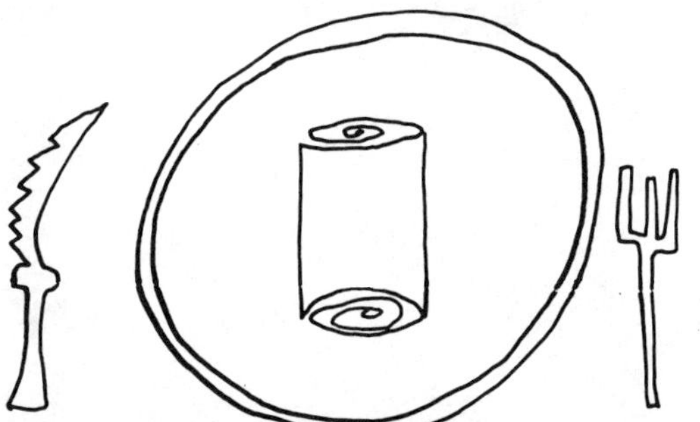
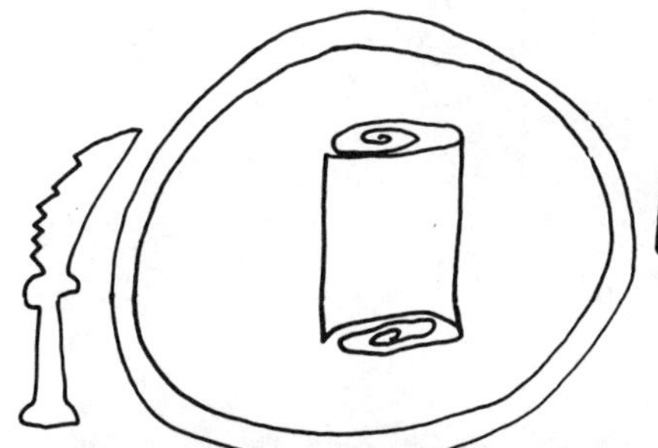

BERRY AND CORN MUFFINS

Preparation and baking time: 30 minutes **Serves 4–6**

These are really fun. You can also make the muffins from a commercial muffin mix. Serve with softened butter.

- 1 1/2 cups all-purpose flour
- 3/4 cup sugar
- 3/4 cup yellow cornmeal
- 1 tablespoon and 1 teaspoon baking powder
- 1/2 teaspoon salt
- 3/4 cup raspberries
- 2 eggs
- 1 cup milk
- 1 teaspoon vanilla
- 4 tablespoons sweet butter, melted

Heat the oven to 400°. Butter and flour twelve 3-inch muffin cups.

Sift together the flour, sugar, cornmeal, baking powder, and salt. Toss the raspberries, rinsed and air-dried, with 1/4 cup of the mixture. With an electric beater, beat the eggs, milk, and vanilla together, and stir into the remaining flour mixture, with the melted butter. The batter will be lumpy. Spoon 2 tablespoons of batter into each muffin cup, and divide the coated berries among the cups. Divide the remaining batter among the cups and bake for 15 to 20 minutes, or until the muffins are golden brown and the tops spring back when lightly pressed.

Variation: Rhubarb-Strawberry Muffins—Follow the method described in the basic recipe, but for the dry ingredients, sift together 1 3/4 cups all-purpose flour, 1/2 cup sugar, 2 1/2 teaspoons baking powder, 3/4 teaspoon salt. For the liquid ingredients, beat together 1 egg, 3/4 cup milk, 1/3 cup melted butter. For the fruit, combine 3/4 cup fresh rhubarb minced in a food processor and 1/2 cup thinly sliced strawberries. Bake the muffins at 400° for 20 minutes or until golden brown. Cool before serving.

STRAWBERRY FRITTERS

Preparation and cooking time: 1 hour **Yield: 20–25 fritters**

By fresh vegetable oil, I mean oil in which nothing has been fried before. This is a special treat—serve the berry fritters as a garnish, on ice cream, for instance.

- 1 pint large firm strawberries
- 1/4 cup Cointreau
- 1/2 cup sugar
- 2 eggs
- 1/2 teaspoon salt
- 1 tablespoon sugar
- 1 tablespoon melted butter
- 2 tablespoons lemon juice
- 1 cup all-purpose flour
- Milk
- 3 cups fresh vegetable oil
- Confectioners sugar

Don't wash the berries unless you really must. And if you must, do it quickly, hull them, drain them, and dry on paper towels in an airy place. Sprinkle with Cointreau and sugar and refrigerate for 1 hour.

Beat together in a bowl the eggs, salt, sugar, butter, and lemon juice, then beat in the flour until well blended. Beat in enough milk to make a batter as thick as heavy cream. Let rest for 20 or 30 minutes.

Heat the vegetable oil to 375° or until a drop of batter sizzles as it hits the fat. Drain the berries, toss with confectioners sugar, coat with batter, and, working with a basket or strainer, lower a few berries at a time into the hot oil. Lift them out as soon as they color—a minute or two—otherwise they will cook to jam. Drain on paper towels and serve at once.

STRAWBERRY SOUFFLÉ

Preparation and cooking time: 1 hour **Serves 4**

This soufflé is made with egg whites rather than whole eggs (see the Raspberry Soufflé on the opposite page). It is exquisitely light and delicious, heavenly served cold with whipped sweetened cream (if any is ever left over). I love its specialness even though I never have an easy time cooking it to the point where it will stay risen long enough to get from the oven to the table. But it's effective even when there's a partial collapse on the way to dinner, and everyone loves the flavor and texture. A 2-quart soufflé mold is essential, along with a collar to increase its height.

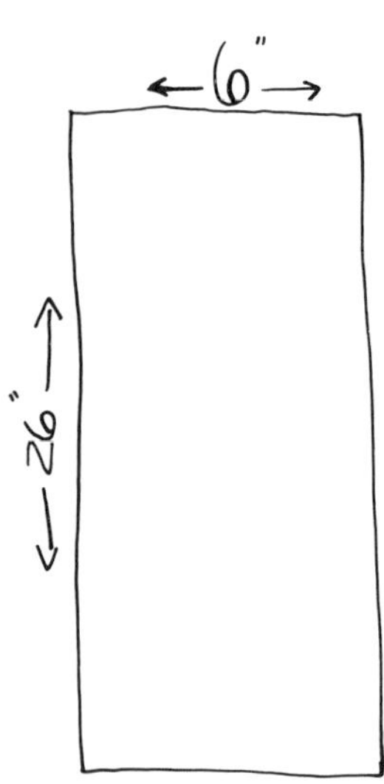

- 8 large eggs
- 2 tablespoons soft butter
- Vegetable oil
- 1/2 cup sugar
- 2 pints ripe strawberries
- 1/2 cup sugar
- 1 tablespoon lemon juice
- 2 tablespoons cornstarch
- 1/4 teaspoon cream of tartar
- 1/8 teaspoon salt
- 3 tablespoons sugar
- 1/2 pint heavy cream
- 2 tablespoons sugar
- 1 tablespoon grated orange rind

Put the eggs into a big bowl filled with hot water.

Butter the soufflé mold well. Cut a 6-inch collar of wax paper long enough to fit around your mold (about 26 inches), oil it on the side to be turned in, and tie it with a string or fix it with tape around the top of the mold. Sprinkle 1/2 cup of sugar around the bottom of the mold, then turn the mold on its side and roll it around to coat the interior and the wax paper with sugar. Toss out any excess left in the bottom.

Preheat the oven to 325°.

Rinse, drain, hull, and dry the berries on paper towels, and puree them in a food processor, a blender, or by hand with 1/2 cup sugar and the lemon juice. Turn the puree into a small saucepan, and over medium heat, bring the berries to simmering. Stir in the cornstarch and cook, stirring, for 2 minutes. Turn off the heat.

Discard the water the eggs warmed in, dry the eggs and the bowl, and separate the whites into the bowl (reserve the yolks to make fresh mayonnaise—you'll find a recipe in *Mad About Fish & Seafood*). With an electric beater on high, beat the whites until they froth, then beat in the cream of tartar and the salt. Continue to beat until the eggs form peaks, then, a teaspoon at a time, beat in the 3 tablespoons sugar. Continue to beat until stiff peaks form. With a rubber spatula, fold the berry puree into the whites, flattening the whites as little as possible. Scrape the mixture into a soufflé dish, set the dish in a pan of boiling water in the preheated oven, and bake for 55 minutes without opening the oven. Remove from the oven and rush to the table.

While the soufflé is baking, whip the heavy cream with the 2 tablespoons sugar and garnish with orange rind. Offer, cold, with the soufflé.

Variation: Raspberry Soufflé—This is made in exactly the same manner as the Strawberry Soufflé but instead of strawberries, use 1 pint raspberries, 1/2 to 3/4 cup sugar with 1 1/2 tablespoons of lemon juice, and a pinch of salt to make the purée. Omit the cornstarch. Use 4 whole large eggs, warmed as described, and separated. Beat the yolks, then beat the puree into the yolks. Beat the whites as in the strawberry recipe, with a pinch of cream of tartar and salt, until they form stiff peaks. Very gently fold the whites into the yolk-and-puree mixture. Pour into the prepared mold and bake set in a pan of hot water in an oven preheated to 350° for 50 to 60 minutes or until set. Serve hot with sweetened whipped cream, or chill and serve cold with whipped cream.

Note: To serve, cut into the hot soufflé with a sharp broad knife or pie server, and use a big spoon and the server to lift the soufflé onto dessert plates.

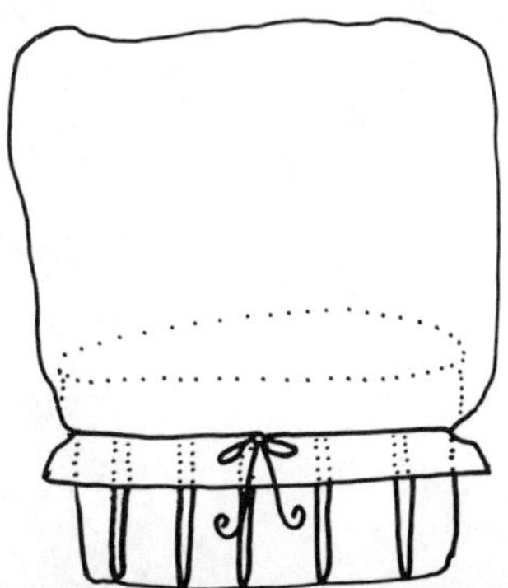

CHOCOLATE BERRY CENTERPIECE

Preparation time: 1 1/2 hours **Serves 4–6**

This small elegant, and delicious centerpiece (even the flowers are edible) doubles as dessert, so it is worth a little time and extravagance. The best strawberries to use are those with long stems, but any big berries with fresh stems will be pretty. Splurge on your favorite fine chocolate, too. For a bowl, I use the type for forcing spring flowering bulbs because the rim turns in and will keep a block of florist's foam in place. You will need a 5″ x 2 1/2″ round bowl and a correspondingly cut piece of foam. A "frog" is a small flower holder: a 4-inch metal one will weight the foam block.

- 2 cups water
- 8–12 ounces bittersweet chocolate
- Pinch of salt
- 1 pint ripe strawberries, hulls and stems on
- 8 drained canned lichee nuts, or chunks of fresh or canned pineapple (optional)
- 1 bunch fresh mint, basil, or parsley
- 4–6 garden pinks or nasturtiums

Several hours before serving, in a small saucepan over low heat, bring 2 cups of water to a boil and place over it a small ceramic or metal bowl containing the chocolate broken into small pieces and the salt. When the chocolate is completely melted, stir once and turn off the heat.

Insert a toothpick into the stem end of each berry, and press halfway into the berry. Set the frog in the bowl and press the florist's foam onto the frog. Holding each toothpick by the end, dip the berry into the chocolate and roll the fruit around to coat all sides. Press the toothpick into the florist's foam. Dip two-thirds of the berries, choosing the least red. Insert toothpicks into the reserved berries and press these into the foam. Refrigerate until serving time.

Before you put the centerpiece on the table, press toothpicks into the lichee nuts or pineapple chunks and set them into the arrangement. Poke mint, basil, or parsley sprigs into the foam around the edge and tuck a few flowers in among the fruits.

THE BERRY FAIRY

MAKING JAMS

I am mad about homemade jams and marmalades, and not at all mad about sterilizing jars and all the rest of the complex process associated with canning. I enjoy putting by jams because the long cooking period sterilizes everything so there is no real need for sterilizing after cooking. Before using, wash jelly and jam jars in the dishwasher, where very hot water and the drying cycle guarantee a high level of cleanliness. I minimize the spoilage hazard by storing the jams and marmalades in the refrigerator: These recipes make small batches so they do not take up much space.

Since the jars don't have to withstand sterilizing in a pressure cooker, I use "found" containers. When a container has no suitable lid, I seal the jam in with melted paraffin (sold in supermarkets).

About cooking jams: they are very easy to make. How perfect they will be—bright in color, almost clear except for the strands of fruit—depends on how well you judge the moment the cooking mass has reached what is called the jelling, or "sheeting," stage. The sheeting stage is the point at which the juice and sugar have cooked enough to jell. This registers on a jelly or candy thermometer at between 218° and 222°. Use a thermometer if you have one, but also check for signs of sheeting. Dip a metal spoon into the boiling fruit; pour the liquid off the spoon back into the pot. When the last two drops clinging to the spoon cling together to form a sheet and drop off slowly, that is sheeting.

Another "doneness" sign to watch for: now and then, after the wildly boiling liquid has simmered down, drag the tip of a spoon across the bottom of the kettle: if it catches, tilt the kettle. If the fruit is jellying and clinging to the bottom of the kettle, the jam is probably cooked. Stir often during the cooking to offset the tendency of sugar to burn on the bottom.

Two other suggestions: when you first start to cook the fruit, juice, and sugar in the kettle, stir the contents of the kettle over low heat until the sugar dissolves. Then raise the heat and boil rapidly, uncovered, to preserve the color and natural flavor of the fruit. Jam cooked too slowly has a too-sugary taste and darkens. Over high heat, the sugar will boil up wildly; that's why you need a big kettle to make even small batches of jam. For making the recipes that follow, I use a 6-quart kettle of heavy aluminum.

RASPBERRY JAM

Cooking and cooling time: 1 hour **Yield: about 2 eight-ounce jars**

This is a basic recipe for making jams without pectin. The kettle should hold about four times as much as the mixture you put into it, so there's plenty of room to boil rapidly. If you have very tart berries, add a generous 2/3 cup of sugar for each cup of fruit puree. The jam is a brilliant color and tastes much like fresh fruit. The late summer berry season is the time to plan on making raspberry jams.

1 quart hulled raspberries
About 1 cup sugar
Pinch of salt

Place the berries in a 4- or 6-quart kettle and mash them. Turn the heat on low, and stir and cook the berries until the juices flow freely. Raise the heat and boil rapidly until the juice looks reduced by half. Measure the fruit and juice; there should be about 12 ounces. Return to the kettle and stir in 2/3 cup of sugar for each cup of puree and the salt. Stir over low heat until the sugar has dissolved, then raise the heat to medium high and boil rapidly. In a few minutes, dip a spoon into the mixture to check for sheeting. Tilt the kettle to see if jelly is forming along the bottom. When doneness signs appear, remove from the heat, cool briefly, and pour into dry, clean jelly glasses. Let cool completely on a rack, then cap or cover with melted paraffin and store in the refrigerator.

BAR-LE-DUC JAM

Dripping time: 4 hours–overnight
Cooking and cooling time: 1 hour **Yield: about 3 eight-ounce jars**

This is my friend Sally Erath's favorite jam. You must have red or a mix of red and white currants to make it, and it is more time consuming than the Raspberry Jam on page 59. But it is considered the most elegant of all the raspberry jams—the epitome of jamness—and worth the effort. Give this away only to close friends with educated palates!

1	pint red currants	4 1/2	cups sugar
1	quart raspberries		

Pick over the currants, but don't remove the stems. Discard spoiled fruit. Mash the currants about a quarter cupful at a time in the bottom of a 6-quart kettle until all are pulpy. Turn the heat to low, cover, and simmer slowly until the currants look white—about 15 minutes. Allow to drip through a dampened jelly bag or cheesecloth bag (wet and doubled) for 4 hours, or overnight, if you prefer.

In the kettle, combine the raspberries and the currant juice. Discard the currant pulp. Slowly, over low heat, stir with the sugar until it is dissolved. Raise the heat and boil rapidly, uncovered, until the mixture begins to thicken. Check frequently for sheeting (see p. 58). Scrape a spoon along the bottom of the kettle now and then to feel for jam sticking, and tilt the kettle to see if jelly is forming on the bottom. When doneness signs appear (see p. 58), remove from the heat. Let the froth die down, stir to mix well, then pour into clean, dry jelly glasses or canning jars. Let cool on a rack, cap, and store in the refrigerator.

STRAWBERRY AND PINEAPPLE JAM

Cooking and cooling time: 1 1/2 hours Yield: about 5 eight-ounce jars

Select the pineapple carefully: It should be ripe enough to be faintly fragrant, but firm. Choose slender, very red rhubarb stalks, and trim them by removing the leaf with an inch of stalk and shaving off the stem end. Choose ripe but firm berries. Stir this jam as little as possible during the cooking to minimize the mashing of the berries. Spring is the season to plan to make strawberry jams.

1/2 fresh pineapple
8 stalks rhubarb, trimmed
5 cups sugar
Pinch of salt
2 pints strawberries

Set the pineapple on a cutting board and cut off the tuft of leaves. Halve the pineapple and put away the half not to be used. With a knife, slice the skin and all the little eyes from the remaining half. Halve it lengthwise through the core, then set each quarter on end and cut away the core. By hand, in a bowl, coarsely chop the pineapple meat. Measure 2 cups of pineapple, including the juice, and pour it into a 6-quart kettle set over low heat. Bring to simmering and allow to bubble gently for 10 minutes.

Meanwhile, slice the rhubarb stalks along their length, then across, to dice them. Measure 2 cups rhubarb and add to the pineapple with 1 cup sugar and the salt. Simmer for 5 minutes, stirring. Pour the remaining sugar into the kettle, stir until it dissolves, then raise the heat and bring to a rapid boil. Rinse and hull the berries and add them to the boiling fruit.

Cook for 25 minutes, tilting the kettle occasionally to see if fruit is jellying on the bottom. Check for sheeting (p. 58). When signs of doneness appear, turn off the heat and pour the jam out into a large, shallow pan to cool. Pour into clean, dry jelly or canning jars. Let them cool completely on a rack, then cap and store in the refrigerator.

STRAWBERRY-WALNUT JAM

Marinating time: 3–4 hours or overnight
Cooking and cooling time: 40–50 minutes

Yield: about 4 eight-ounce jars

I sometimes think I make this for the pleasure of watching the foaming syrup rolling like pink clouds at the bottom of the jam kettle. Then I think I make it because I also am mad for the exotic flavor of cardamom. If you can't find cardamom at your local supermarket, try a shop specializing in Far Eastern foods or write to Gillies 1840, at 160 Bleecker Street, New York, NY 10012; (212) 260-2130. They have everything, including extraordinary coffee beans of every sort and a historic reputation.

- 3 pints firm ripe berries
- 5 cups sugar
- 2 1/2 teaspoons ground cardamom (optional)
- 1/3 cup strained lemon juice
- 1 1/2 cups broken walnut meats

Rinse, drain, and hull the berries, and in the bottom of a big jam kettle (at least 6 quarts), layer the berries with the sugar mixed with ground cardamom, if you are using it. Let stand for 3 to 4 hours or overnight.

Over low heat, bring the berries and sugar to a simmer. Watch to make sure the fruit and sugar don't burn, but stir as little as possible to keep the fruit whole. Instead, shake the pan briskly over the heat if some portions seem to be bubbling too quickly. When the sugar has dissolved, raise the heat to medium and bring to a full, rolling boil. Add the lemon juice. Cook rapidly for 12 to 15 minutes, then tilt the pot to see if there are signs of jellying along the bottom. Check for sheeting (see p. 58). When signs of doneness appear, remove from the heat, stir in the walnuts, shake the kettle to mix the walnuts into the jam, then pour the jam out into a wide, shallow pan to cool completely. Pour into dry, clean jelly jars, cap, and store in the refrigerator.

RHUBARB-STRAWBERRY MARMALADE

Marinating time: overnight
Cooking and cooling time: 1 hour

Yield: about 6 eight-ounce jars

This is my favorite strawberry preserve—it looks great, and it is loaded with golden raisins and walnuts as well as the fresh fruits. It's tart and yummy and great for giving away—if you do, give the recipe with it. A recipe for spring.

- 1/2 large lemon
- 1/2 large orange
- 1 lime
- 2 packed cups rhubarb pieces 1 inch long (about 5 or 6 stalks)
- 2 cups hulled strawberries (about 1 1/2 pints)
- 4 cups sugar
- 1/2 cup golden raisins
- 1/2 cup walnuts

Juice the citrus fruits and discard the seeds. Reserve the juice. Place the skins in a small enamel or glass saucepan, cover with water, and simmer for 15 minutes, uncovered. Drain, and discard the water. Cool the skins under running cold water, and with a sharp small spoon, scoop out all the white pulp and discard. With scissors, cut the peels into *very* thin strips. In a large bowl, combine the citrus juice, citrus peel, rhubarb, berries, sugar; cover and marinate overnight.

Place the fruit in a big kettle. Over low heat, bring to a simmer. Shake the pan briskly if it is bubbling too quickly. When the sugar has dissolved, raise the heat to medium and bring to a full, rolling boil. Cook for 10 minutes, add the raisins, and boil 5 minutes more. Tilt the pot to see if there are signs of jellying along the bottom. Check for sheeting (see p. 58). When signs of doneness appear, remove from the heat, stir in the walnuts, shake the kettle to mix the ingredients, then pour out into a wide, shallow pan to cool completely. Pour into dry, clean jelly jars, cap, and store in the refrigerator.

RECIPE LIST / INDEX